# The Underground Sketchbook of Tomi Ungerer

**FANTAGRAPHICS BOOKS**

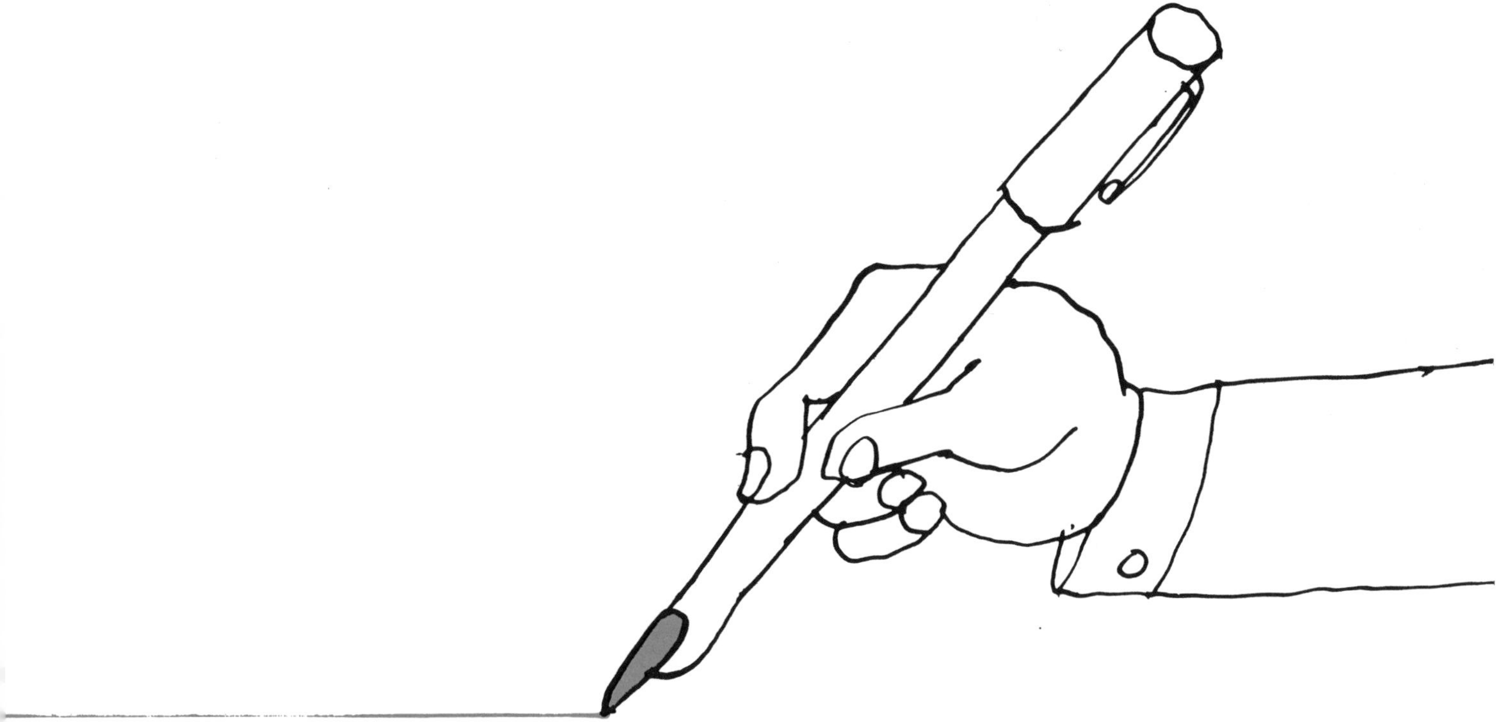

*The Underground Sketchbook* is the first volume in
Fantagraphics' publishing program to reprint Tomi
Ungerer's classic works and to introduce them to a
new generation of readers. Future editions will include
*The Party*, *Adam & Eve*, and *Bablyon*.

# INTRODUCTION BY
# STEVE BRODNER

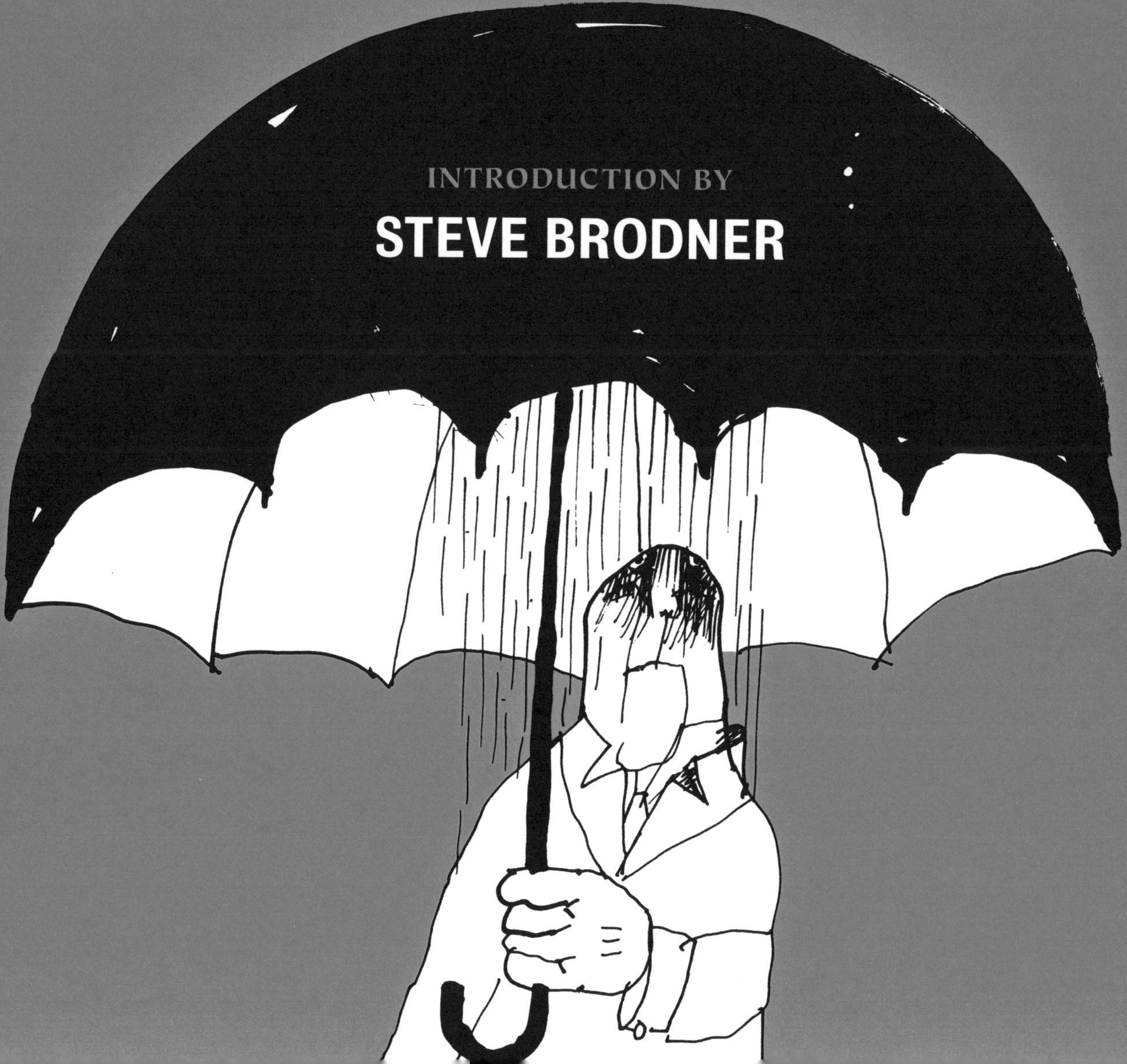

WHEN THE WORLD LOST TOMI UNGERER ON FEBRUARY 9, 2019, it found itself without the wittiest, strongest voice it had in the graphic arts. Tomi was its Renaissance man, in whom the times, the skills and the man all met in a 60-year explosion of humorous, politically uncompromising, sexually candid graphic magic. Tomi always held onto the memory of himself as the little boy of Nazi-occupied Alsace, who knows that politics is not a mass entertainment. He also, somehow, preserved that child's vision of the world as he created over 100 books that will continue to delight kids everywhere. There was the young adult who saw the coming of the sexual revolution. And the graphic artist who saw a path blazed by Saul Steinberg that told him to explore the mysteries in simultaneously stripping down work to its most primitive elements while telling the most sophisticated stories.

He arrived in NY in the early '60s, when print was king. What appeared in papers and magazines then mattered very much to readers. America's best writers crafted pieces for *Esquire, Playboy, The New Yorker, Holiday, Collier's, New York, Saturday Review, Life, Look, The New York Times*, etc. And the artists held similar sway, as famous as TV stars today. They were all deeply talented at the start and then, with print success, became even greater: Charles Addams, Al Hirschfeld, Milton Caniff, Walt Kelly, Bill Mauldin. Al Capp, Herblock, David Levine, Milton Glaser, Ed Sorel, Saul Steinberg, James Thurber, etc. Into this world walked Tomi. Over a short time, he realized an alchemy as never before seen: how to speak in a common graphic language that was warm, welcoming and sharp as a razor.

I knew Tomi's work first from the political posters of the anti-war and civil rights eras. They were immediate, relevant and very clarifying and right at the tip of the spear of our political moment. Only later did I become aware of his erotic art. These books show a torrent of ideas, many of the most arch, sexual kind. From the perspective of our more accepting times, I can only imagine the shock that greeted these. Certainly moms who were eagerly awaiting the next Ungerer children's book were deeply aggrieved; some, perhaps, finding out the true nature of the books a bit too late. Today those kids, grown and worldly, would find these small moments of human perversion and world-wise human debasement a refreshing discourse on our various selves at our ongoing inner battlefields. And it is bloody. The only other color we get here is red and it is not just used for lipstick.

If the jokes are funny it must be said that they are told from the point of view of a male of his generation. Women have power here; not of the political kind, but in being the beneficiaries of the unmistakable power of nature. It is the power to torment, to kill. The woman with the magnet between her legs is having fun, perhaps not entirely aware of how helpless men are in her presence. It is a strict binary paradigm, one that might seem out of place in a world of awakening consciousness of relationships from more than one perspective. Also being "woke" about sex means understanding the ever-widening rainbow of pansexual discourse. You won't find any of that here. It all must be taken in the context of the Mad Men era when a joke was for the traditional audience: one comfortable in its understood white-male place on top. She is capable of keeping a poor deflated man on the wall for her use at will. She pulls organs out of his mouth and displays them on a table. She uses him as a showerhead as she lies happily in the tub. She is an immense prize fighter moving in for the kill, while the ropes are made of barbed-wire. But there is a constant reminder that, for the man, this is the price that will be paid for attending your desires … or refraining from them. It is more a resigned recognition of the power of libido, rather than any liberation asserted by women. For Tomi it is all trouble all the time. Fatal but not serious. Pointy-breasted eye-poker is coming for you and will severely cut you for your trouble. She is the black widow spider who bites the head of its mate upon climax and eats the rest of him for dessert. The howling woman is seen floating aloft with fish hooks in her mouth and genitals.

I think that the idea of the persecuted man here is in the context of man's own self-destructive tendencies. He is a melting candle, where the head is a lit candle wick, working its way down toward self annihilation. He is a nerd caressing a lit bomb. He pours water into his own boat. He walks around encased in his own small prison.

The hopeless relationships between man and life's hierarchies, especially with the military, do not get overlooked. These are, in a broad sense, political drawings. A smiling man plays the xylophone using the heads of his subordinates. Men's heads are being popped off of bodies like corkscrews. Soldiers march with grave markers instead of guns. The general wears a ribbon made of a small man who has hanged himself. The photographer of an A-bomb explosion (one can see under the cloth) is, himself, a skeleton.

Strangely, as fatal as many of these images are, the attack and humor is one of unmistakable joie de vive. The line weight is at once controlled and out of control. And therefore crackles with life, more than the more controlled Steinberg's. The characters are drawn as direct in-your-face portraits of the naked id, pulsing with the vibration of recognition of the sad truth of life—and you laugh your ass off.

The next to last piece sums up the book, and maybe, in a sense, even Tomi himself. A man and a woman are on train tracks making love, with the train fast approaching. Here, knowing the end is nigh but also knowing that, right now, living in the moment is the only thing that matters. Death is inevitable and, maybe, no big deal; the joy of life, for all the misery involved, is worth the whole damned thing.

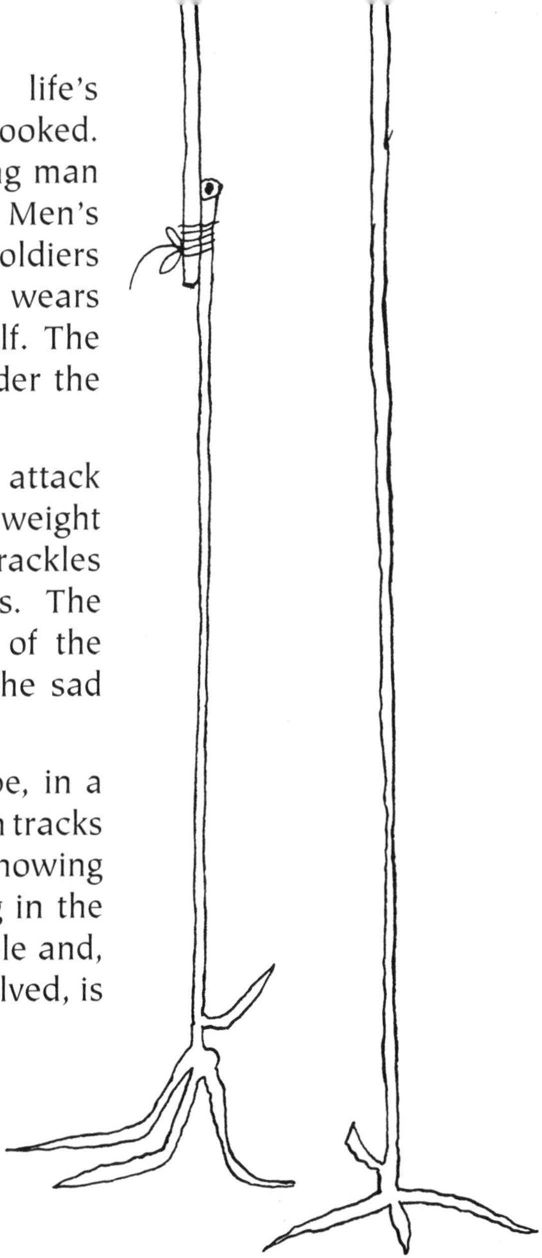

—SB

The Underground
Sketchbook

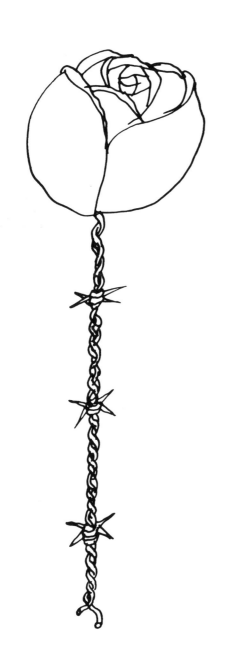

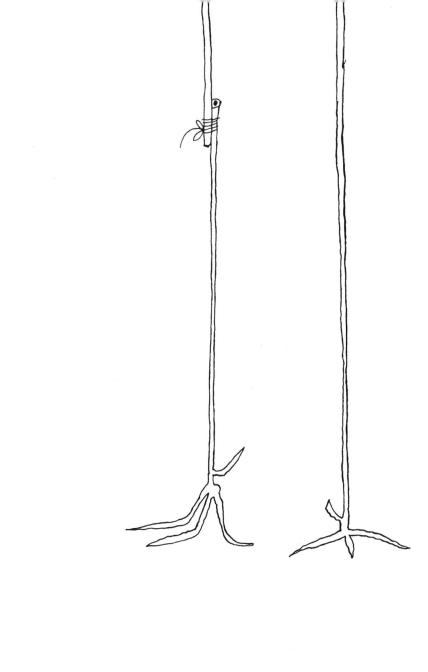

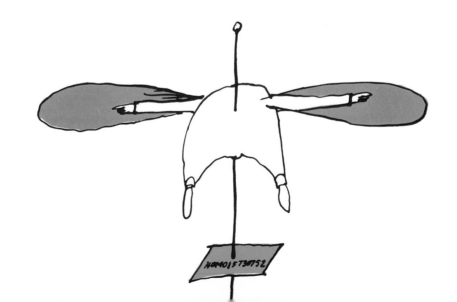

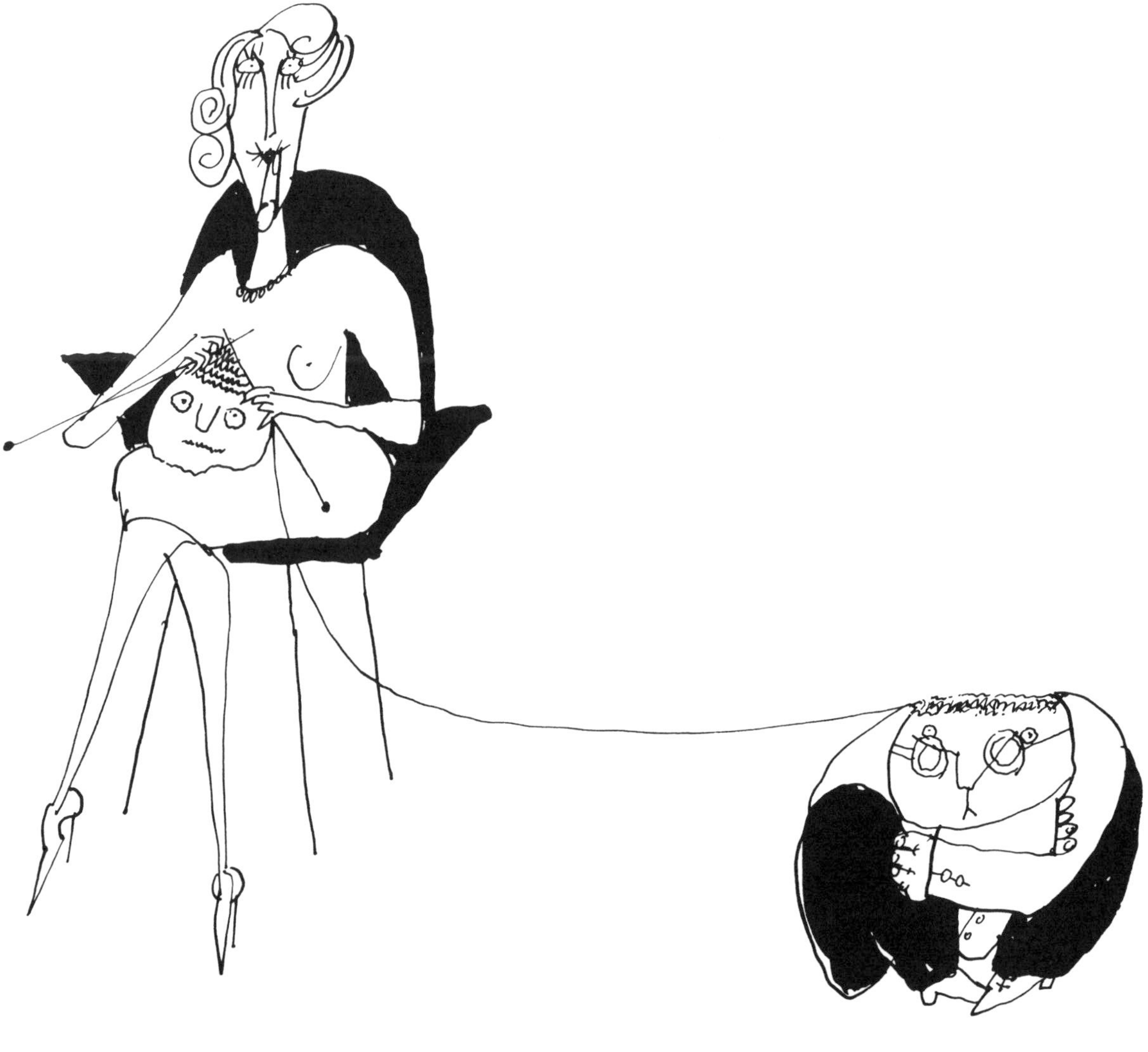

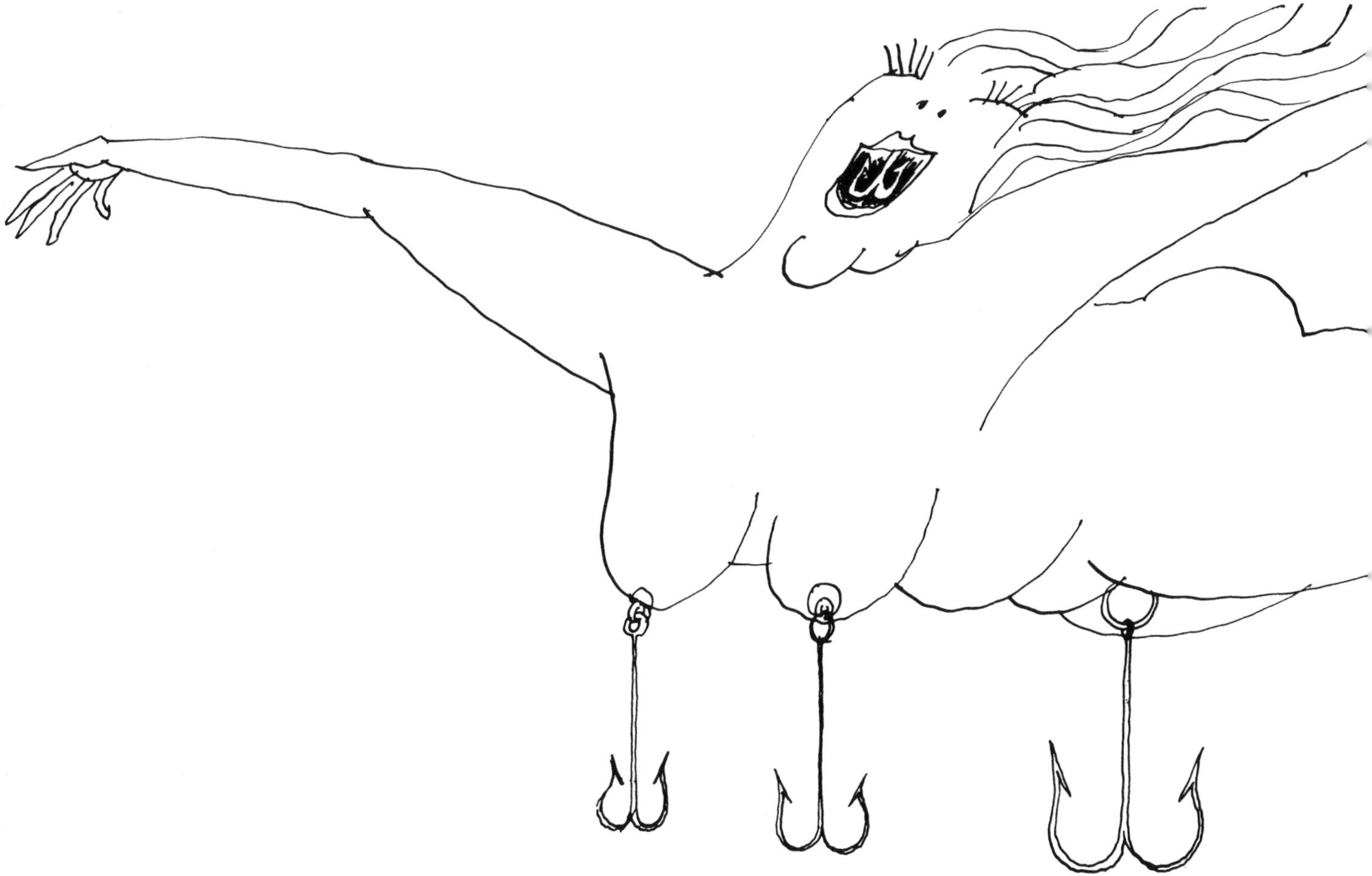

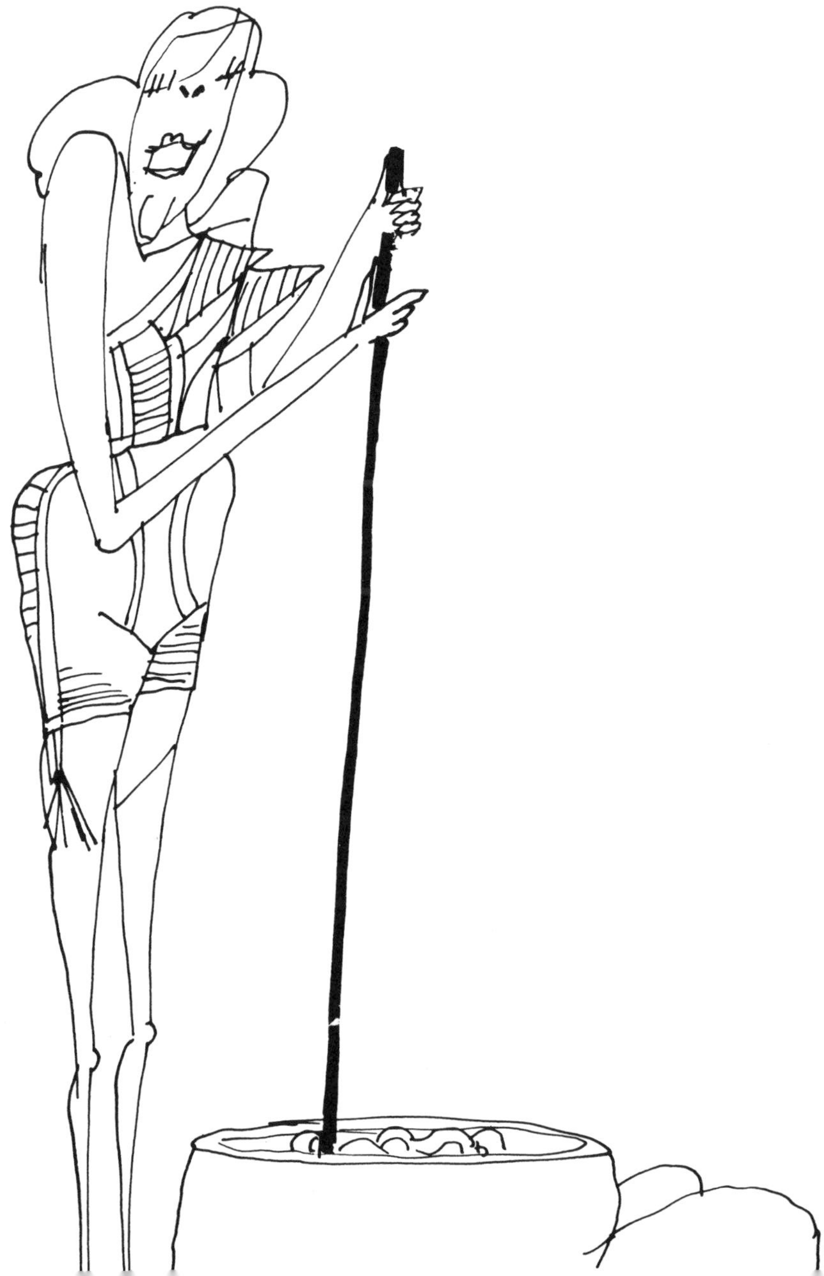

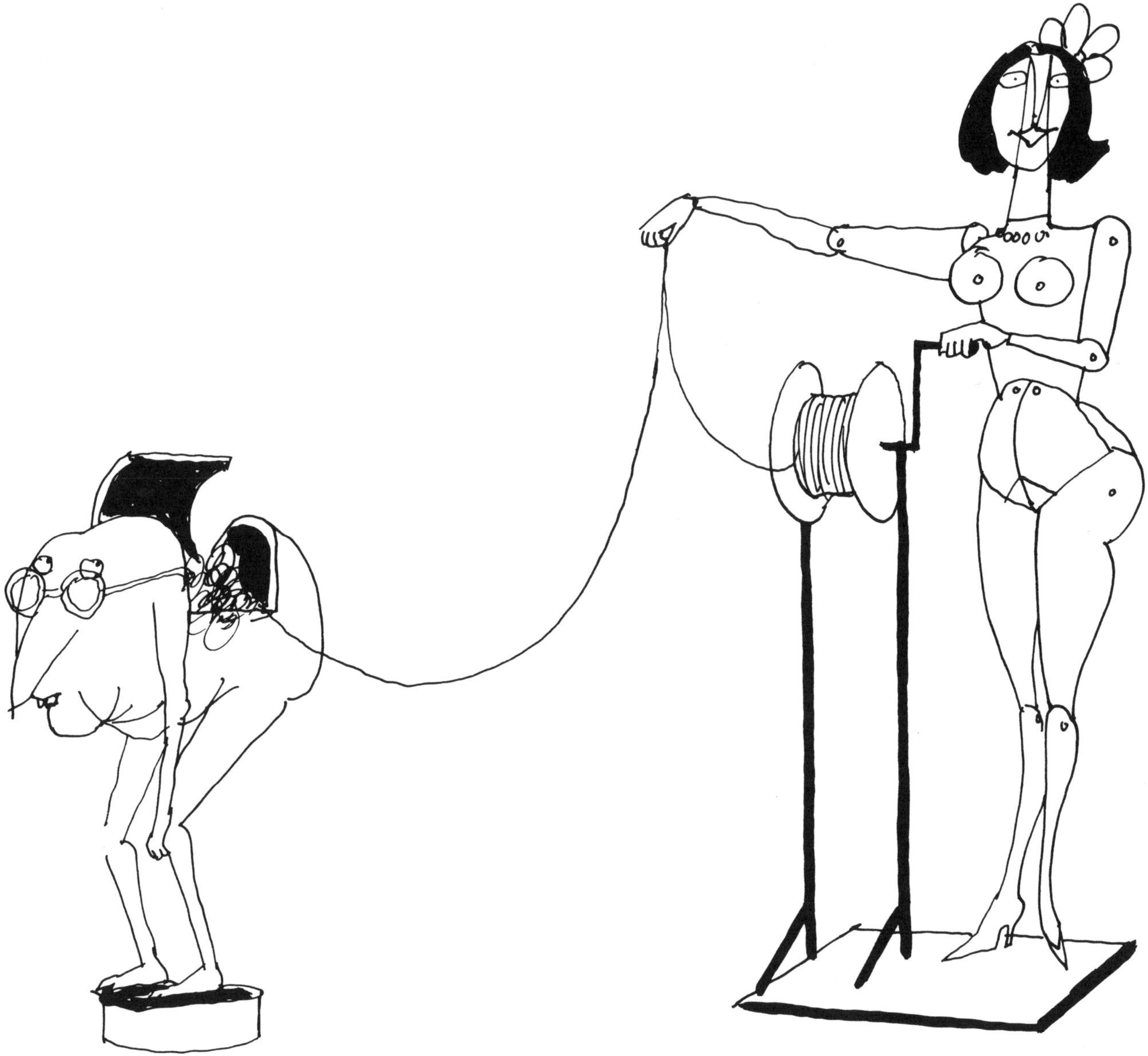

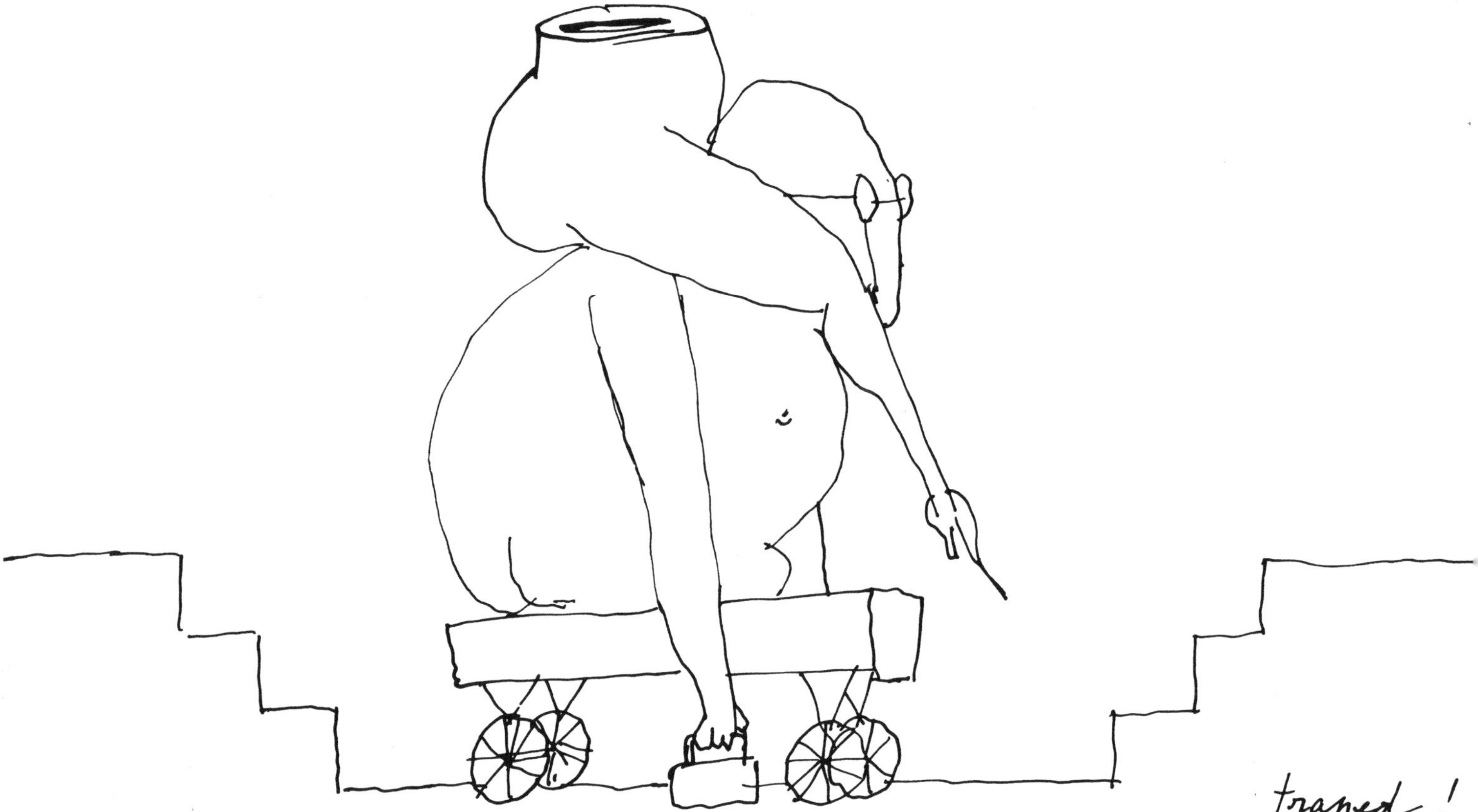

traped !

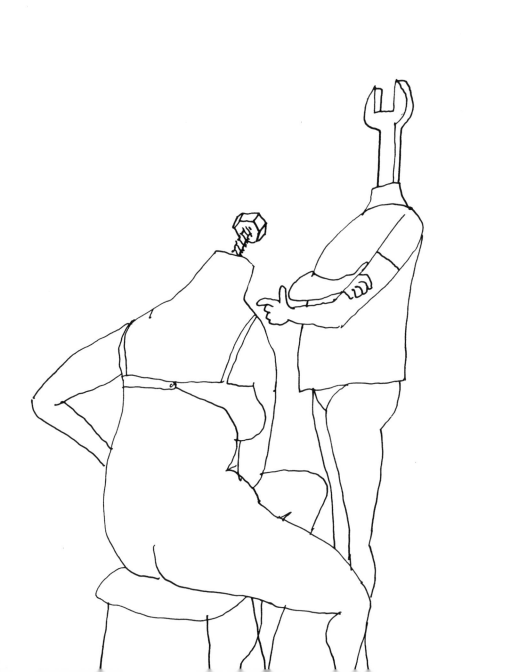

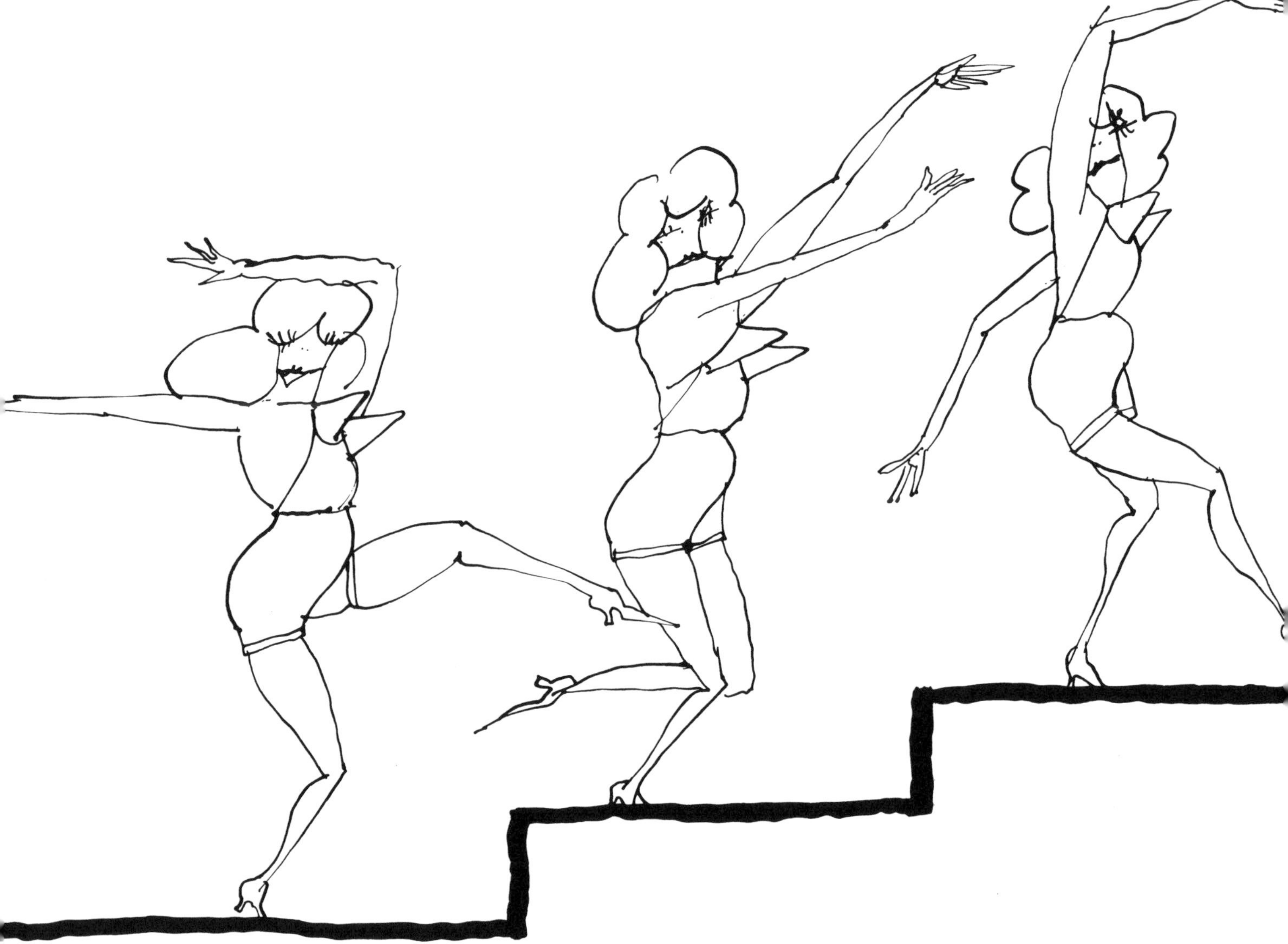

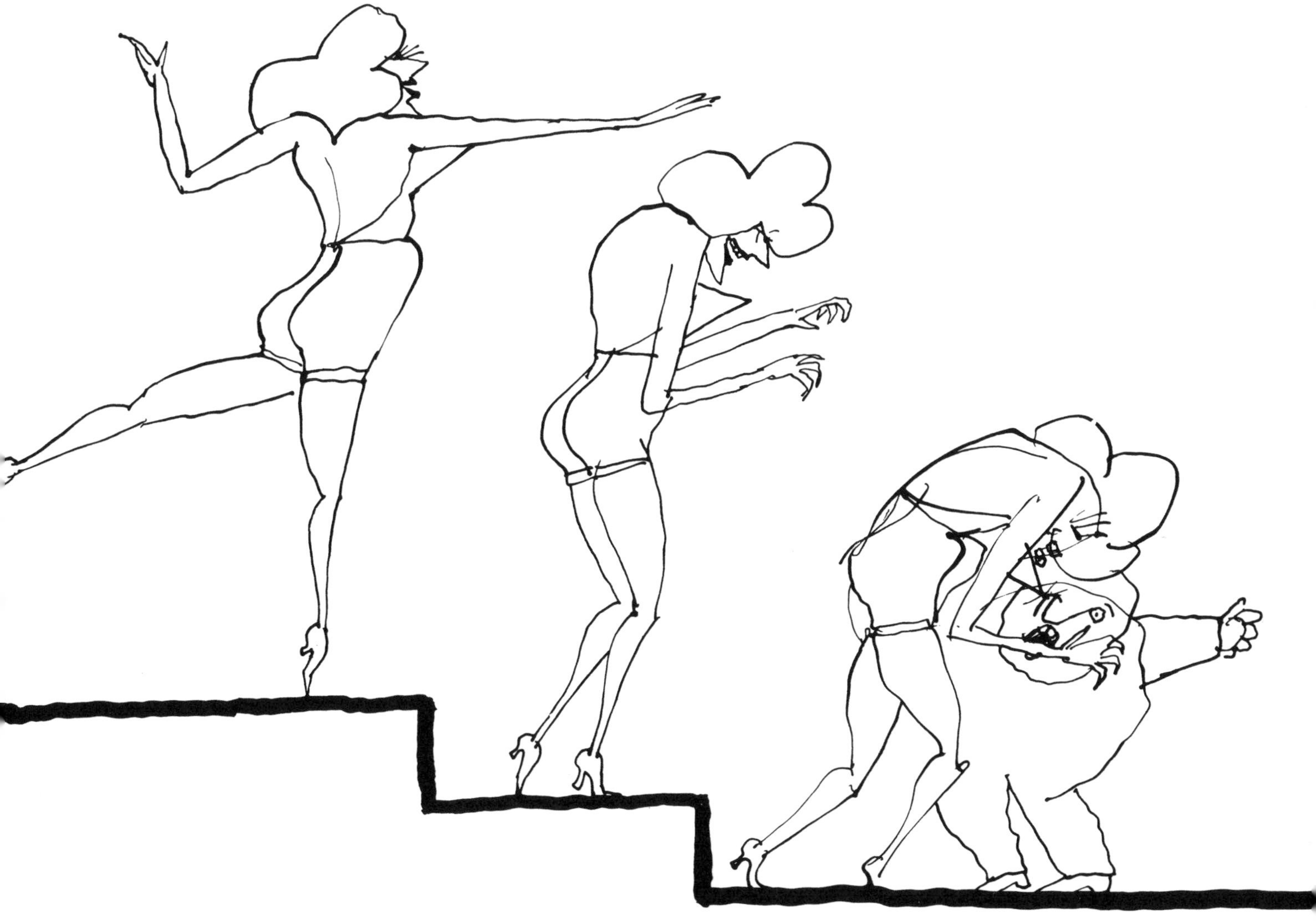

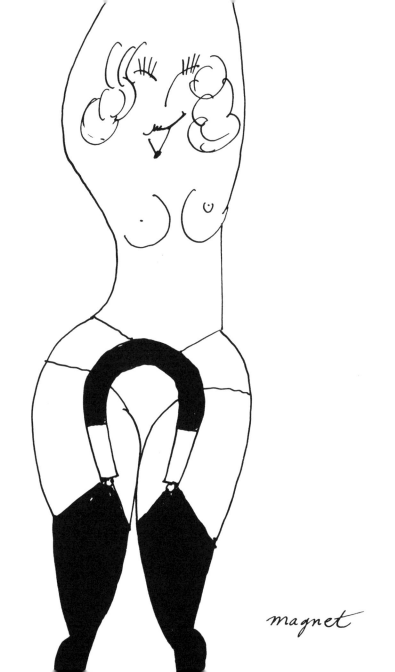

magnet

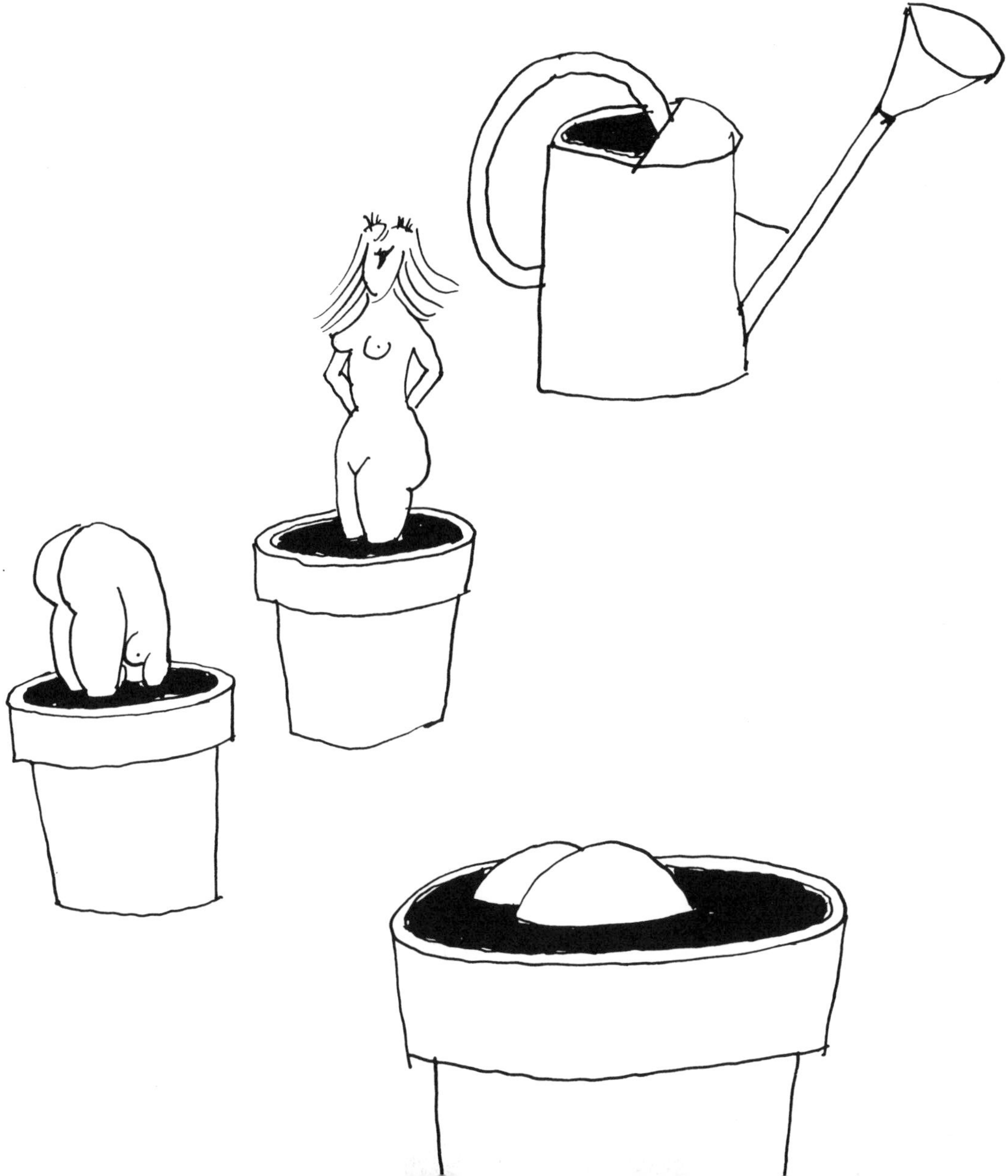

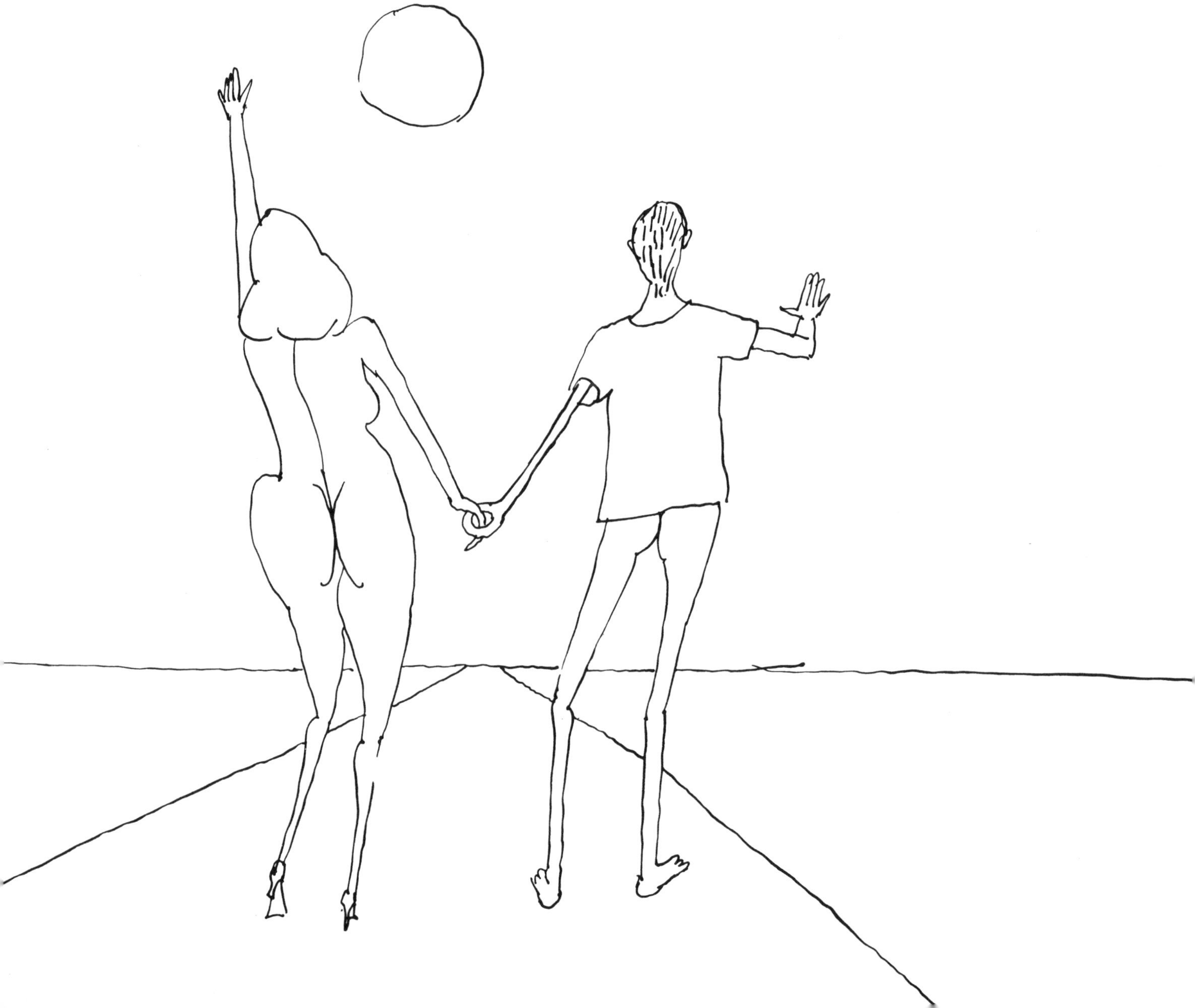

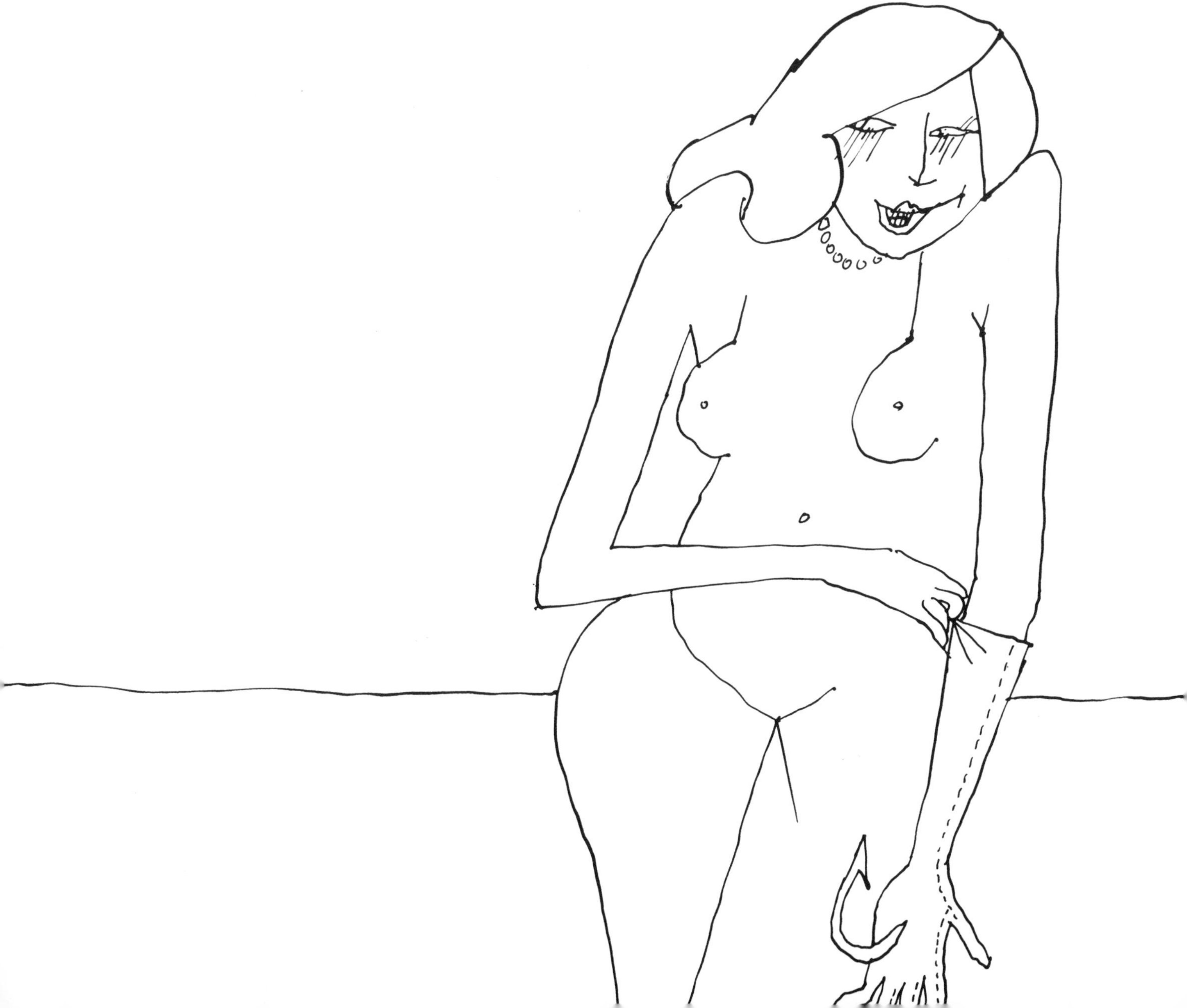

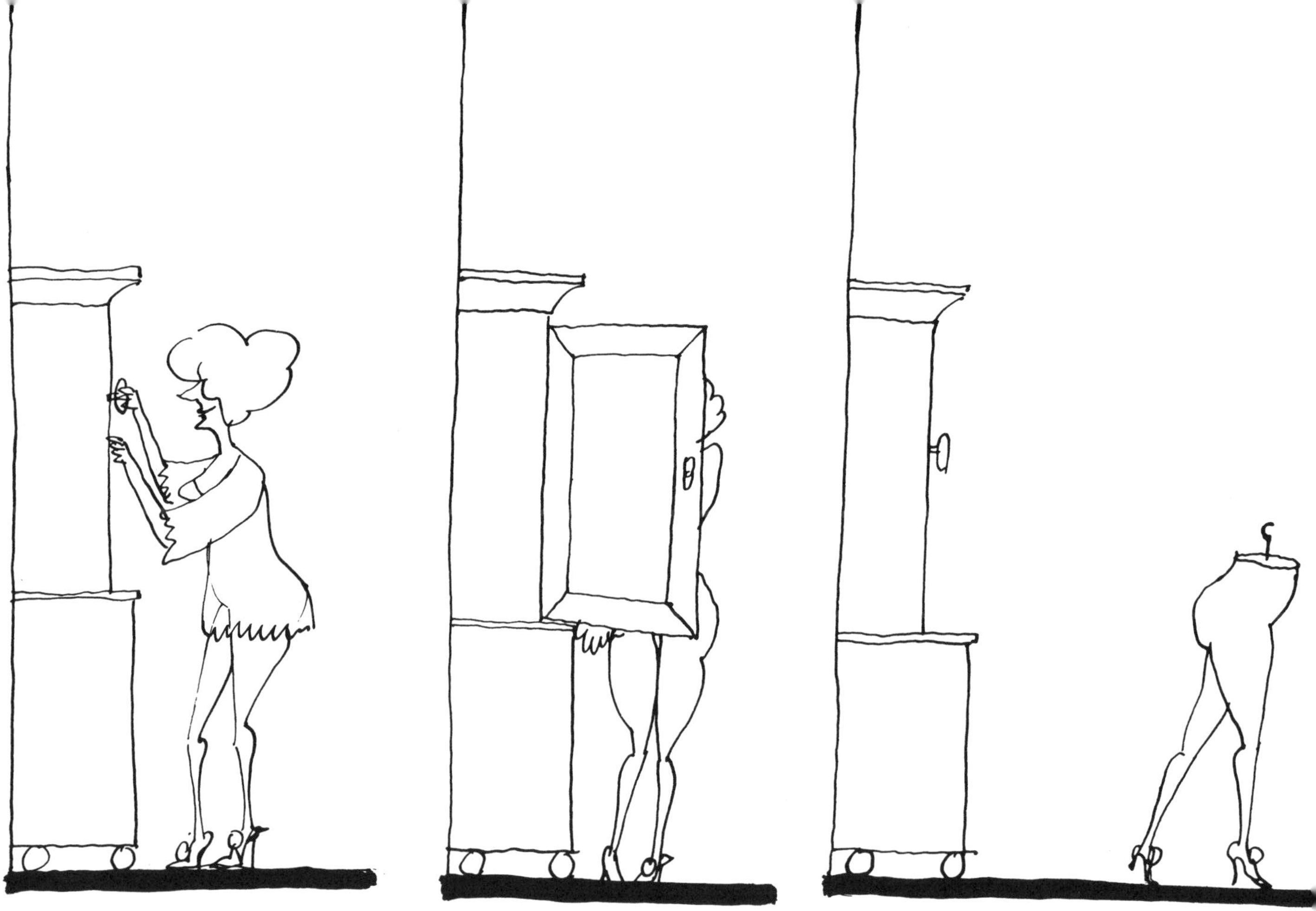

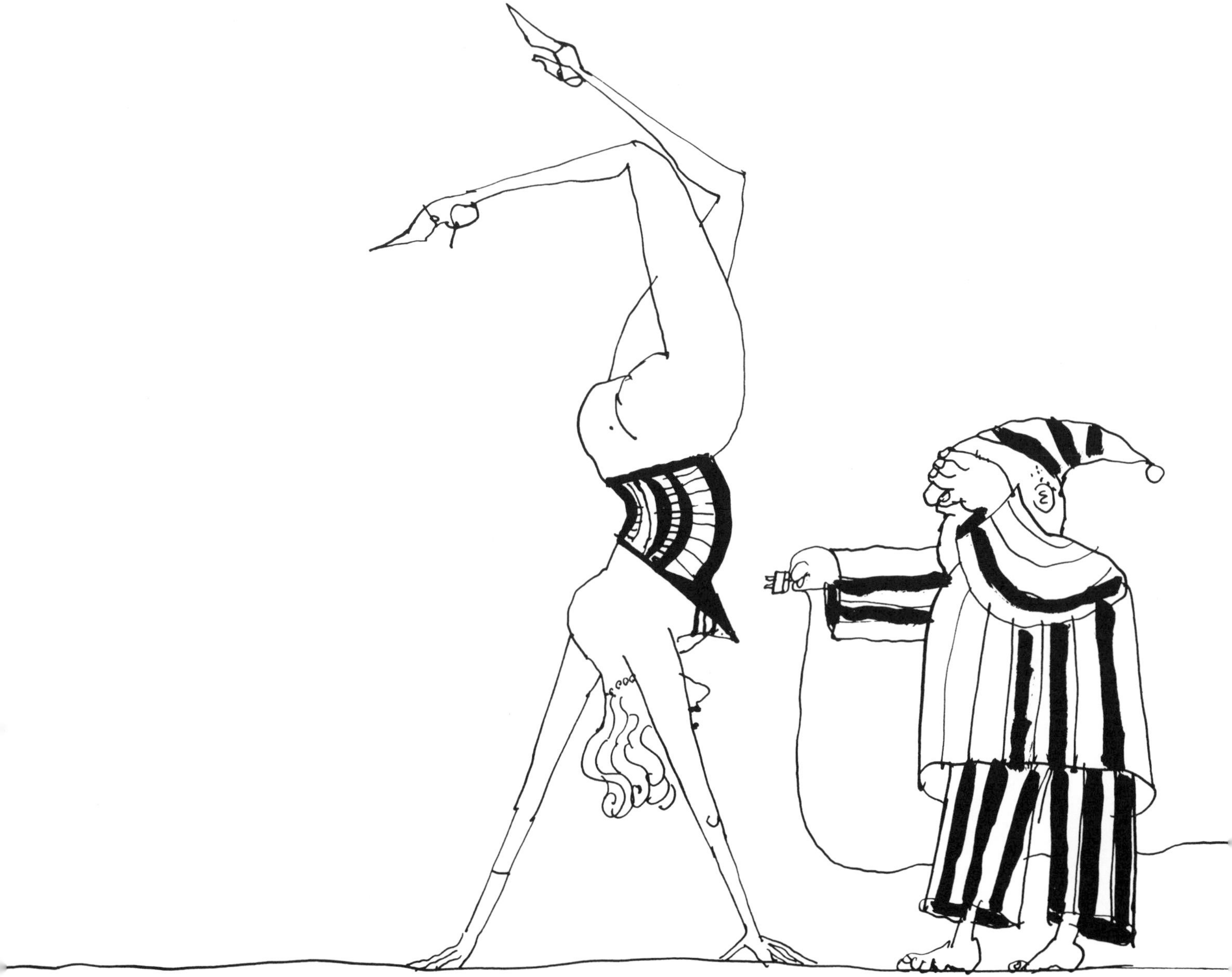

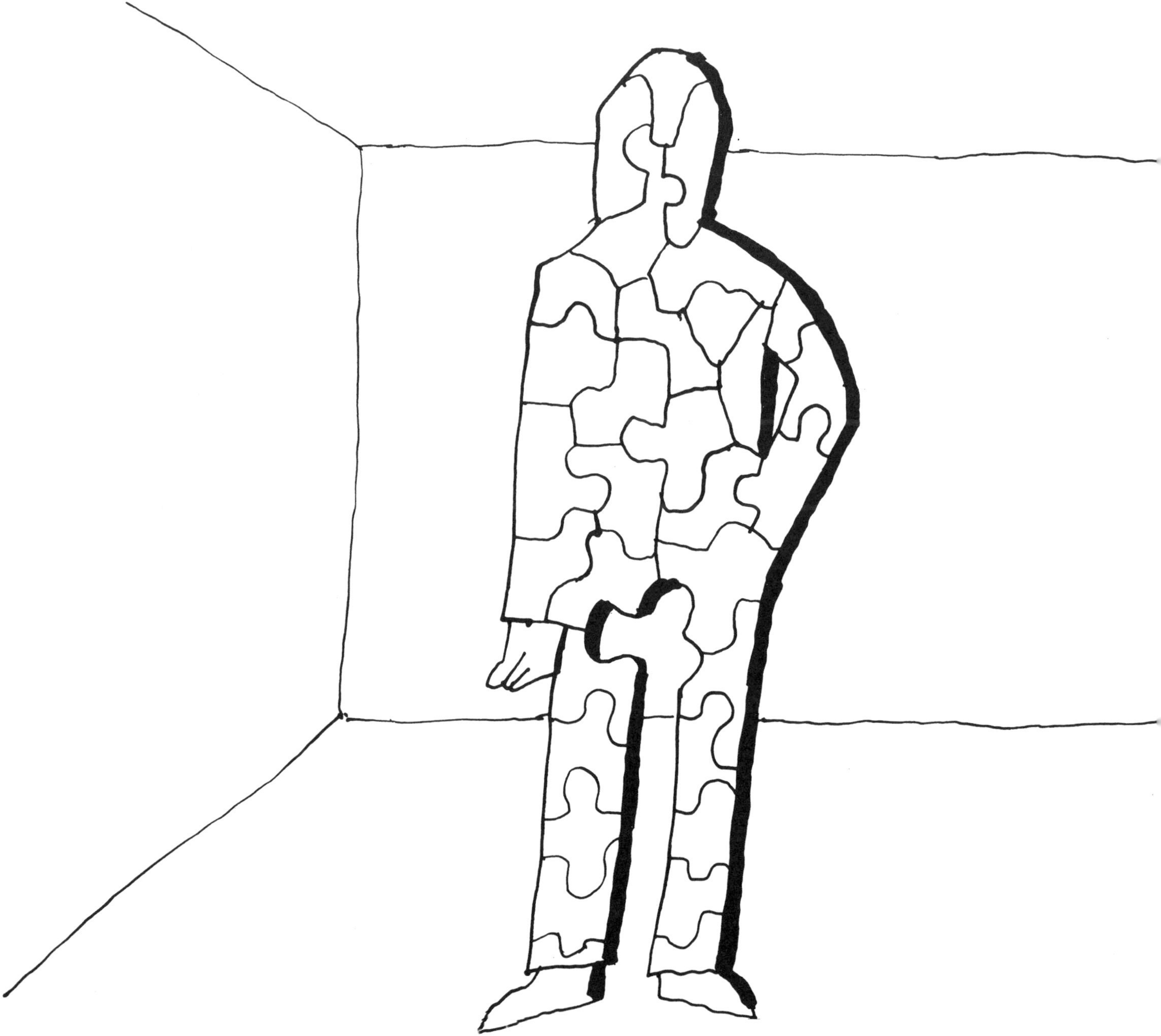

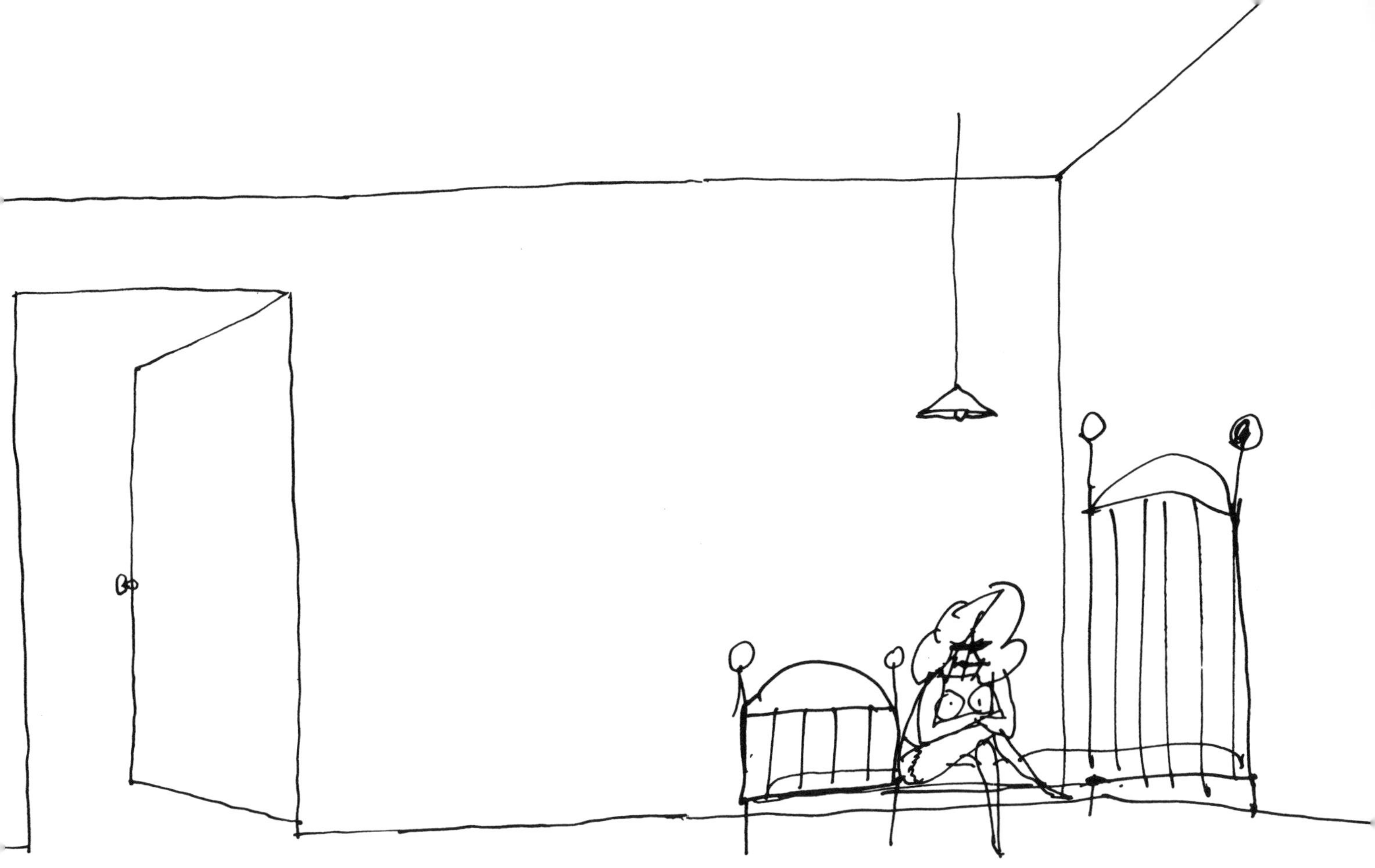

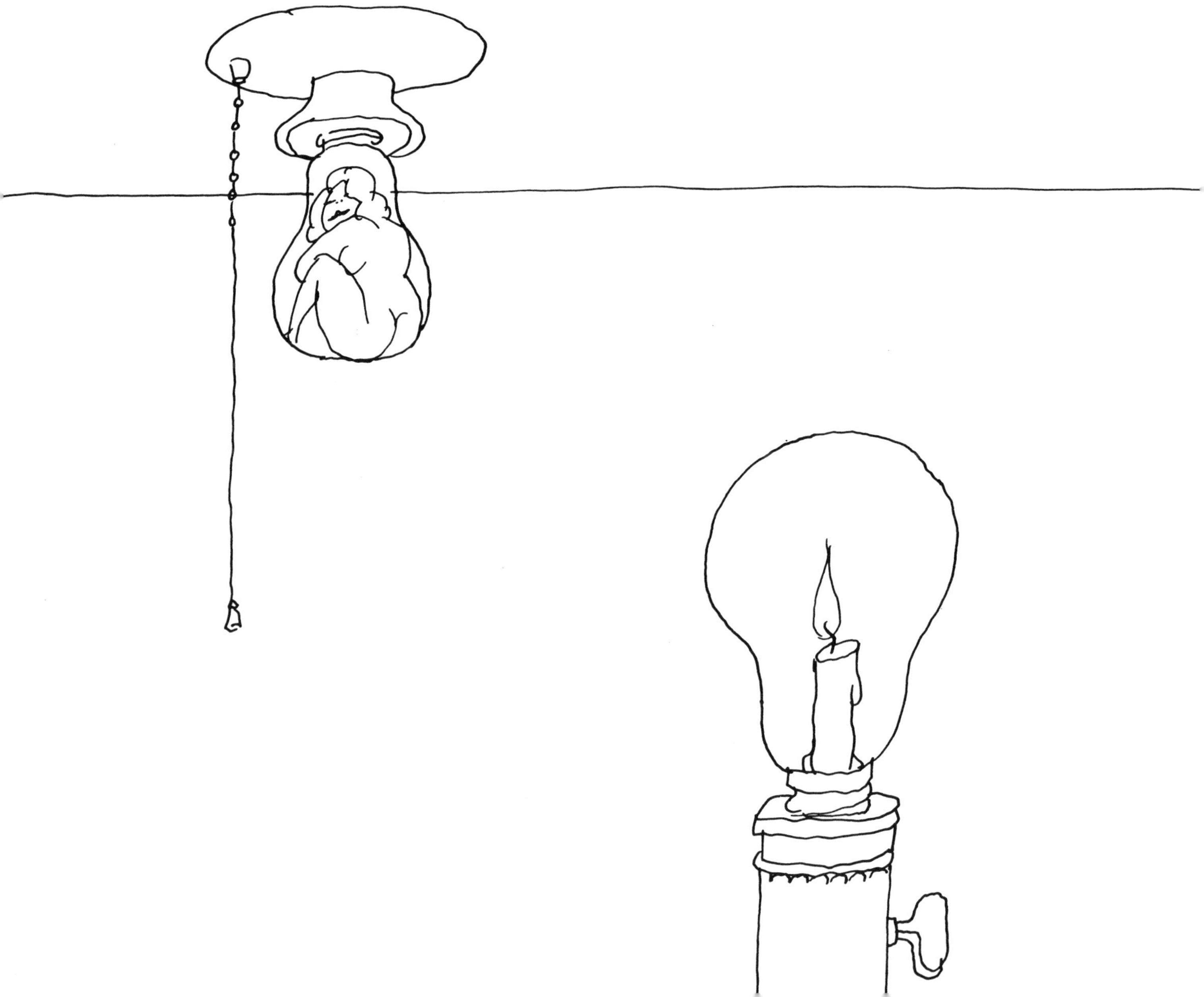

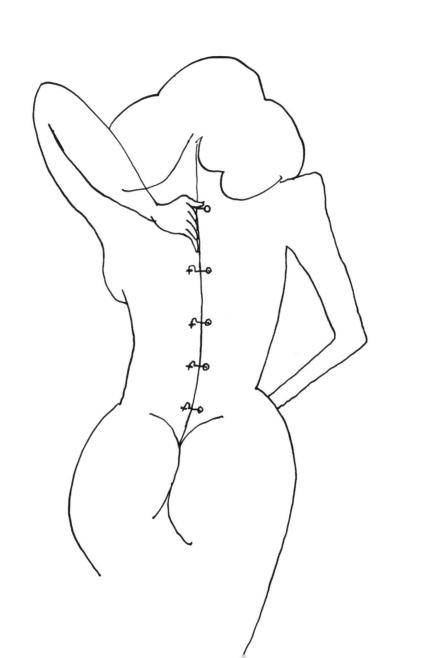

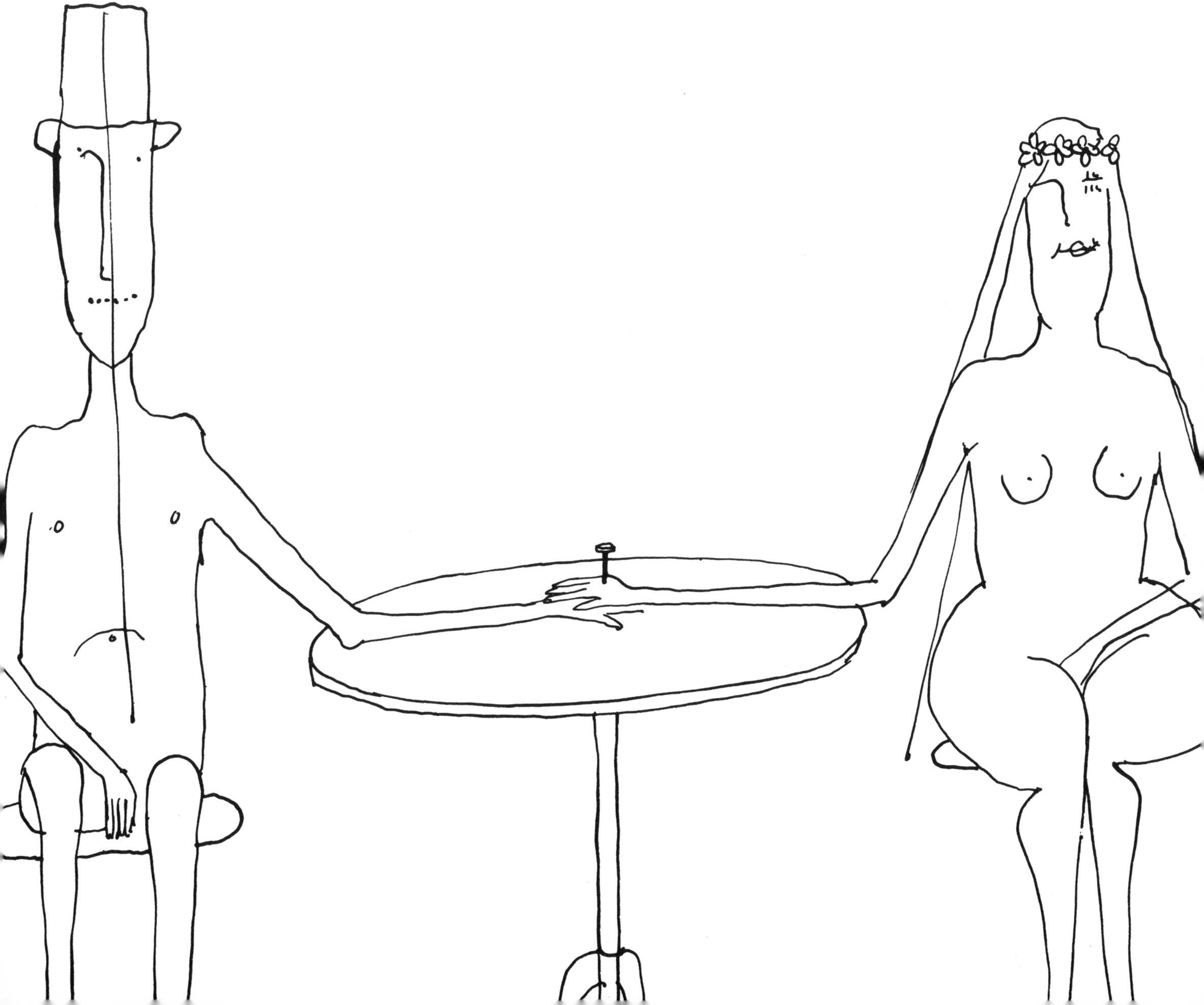

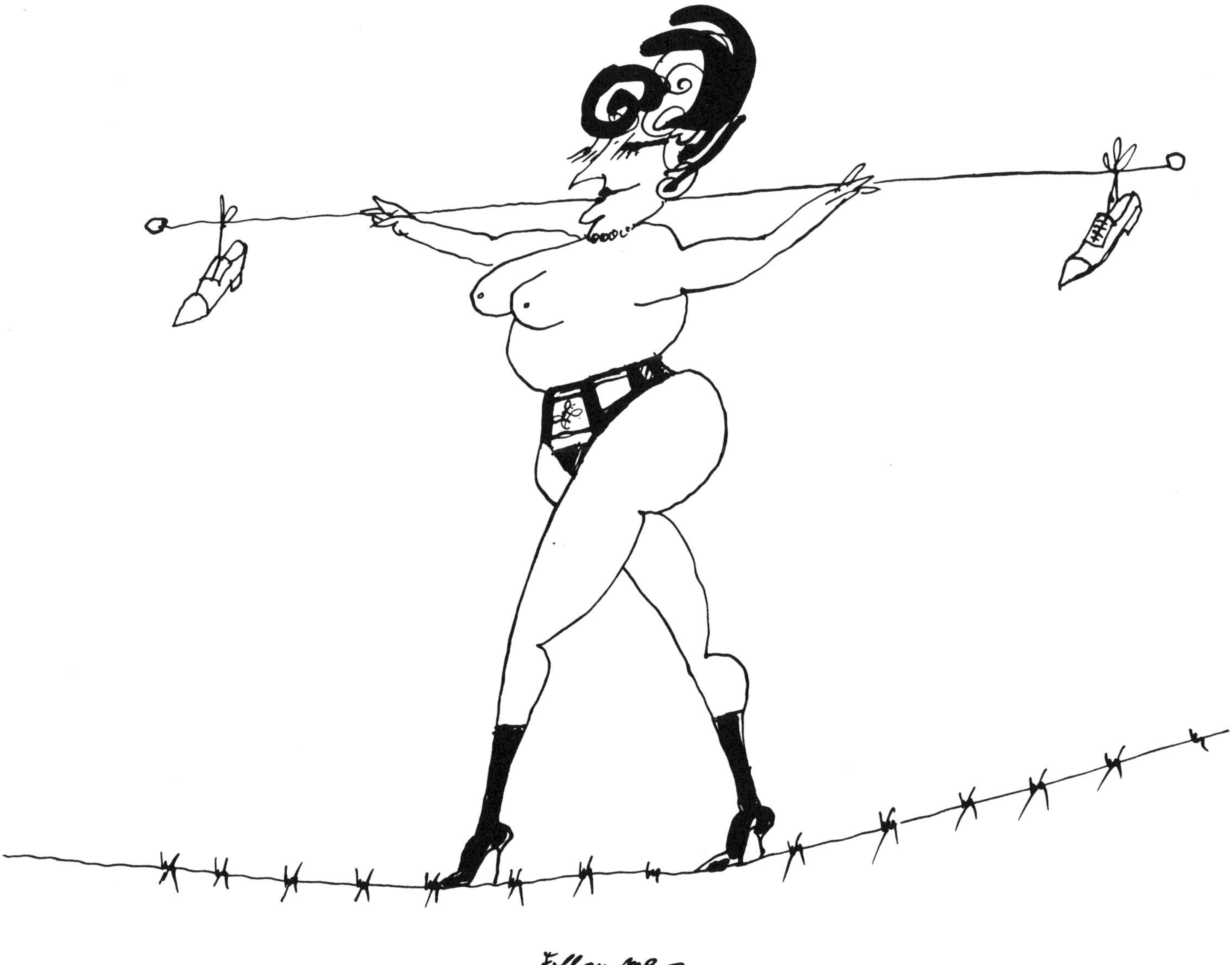

*Follow me*

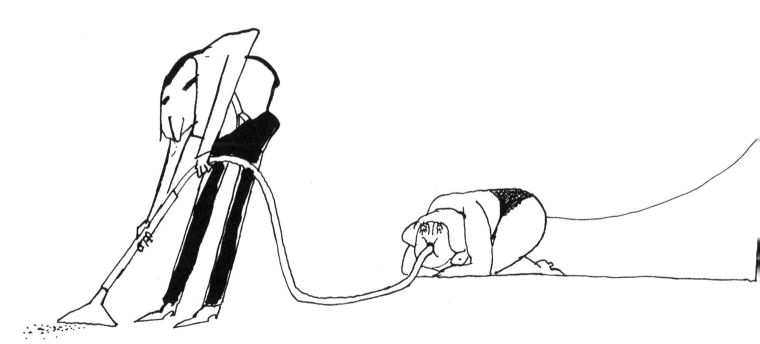

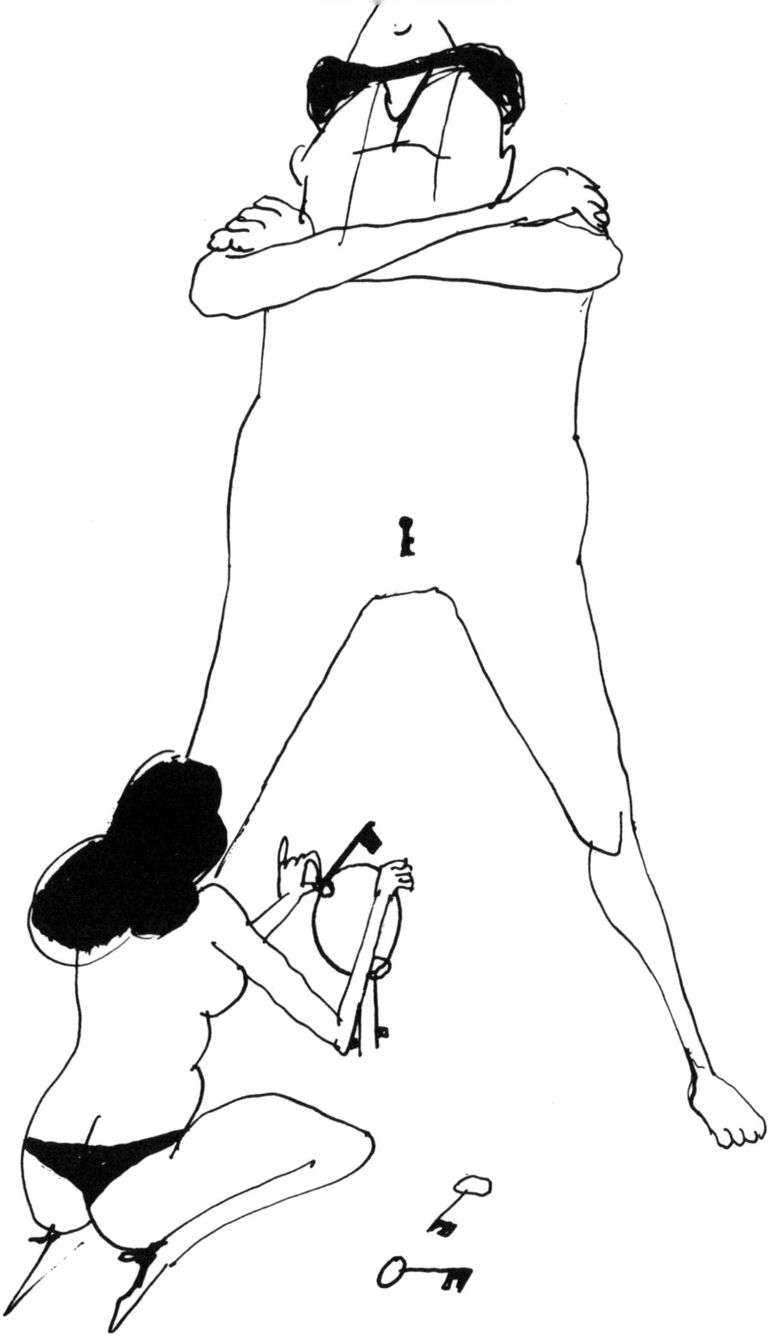

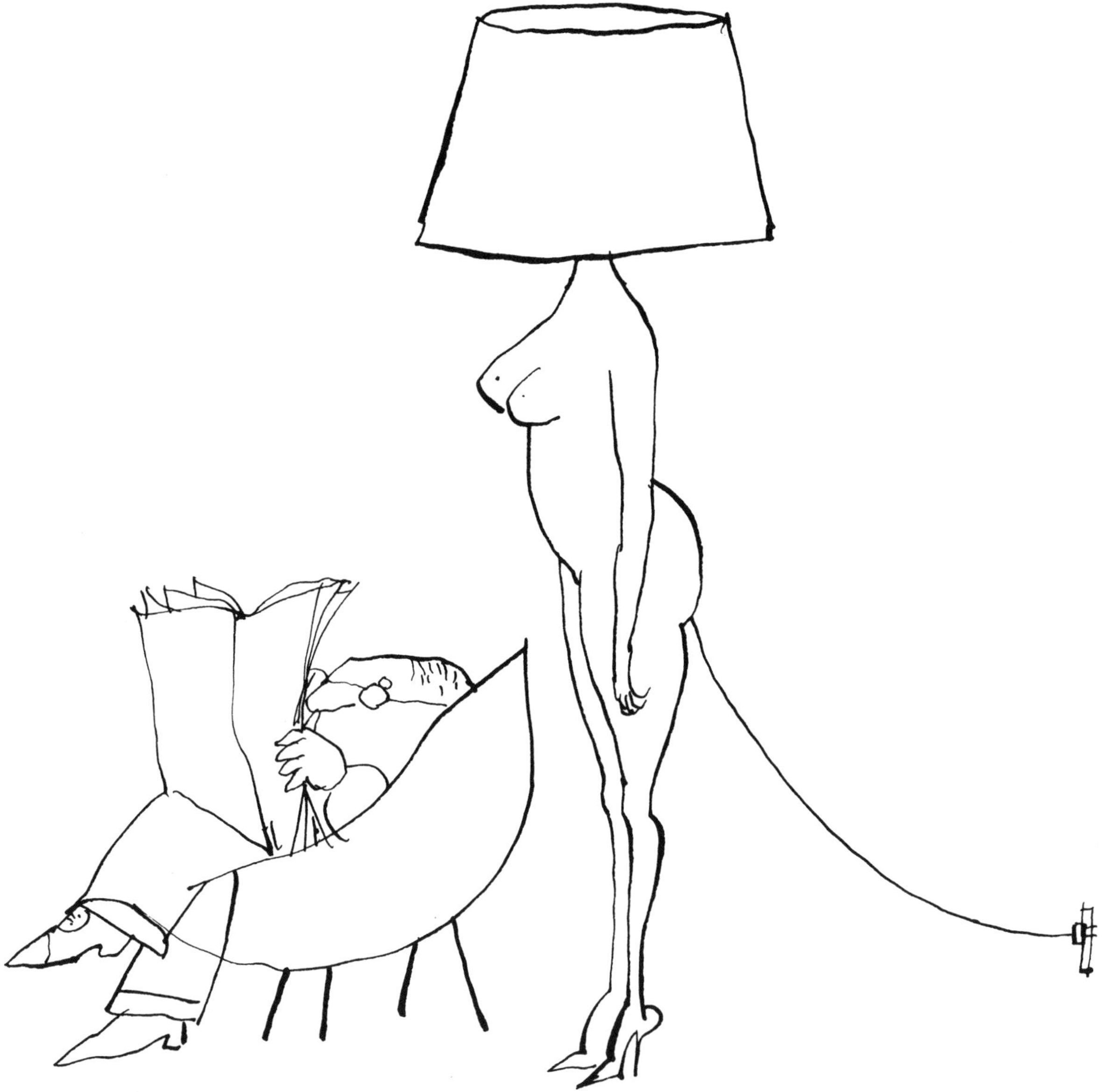

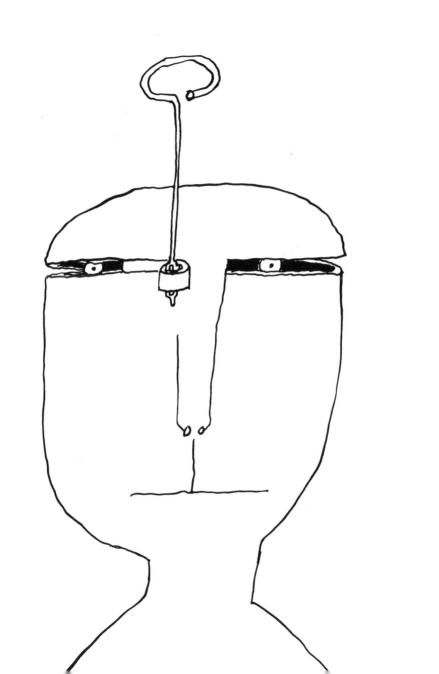

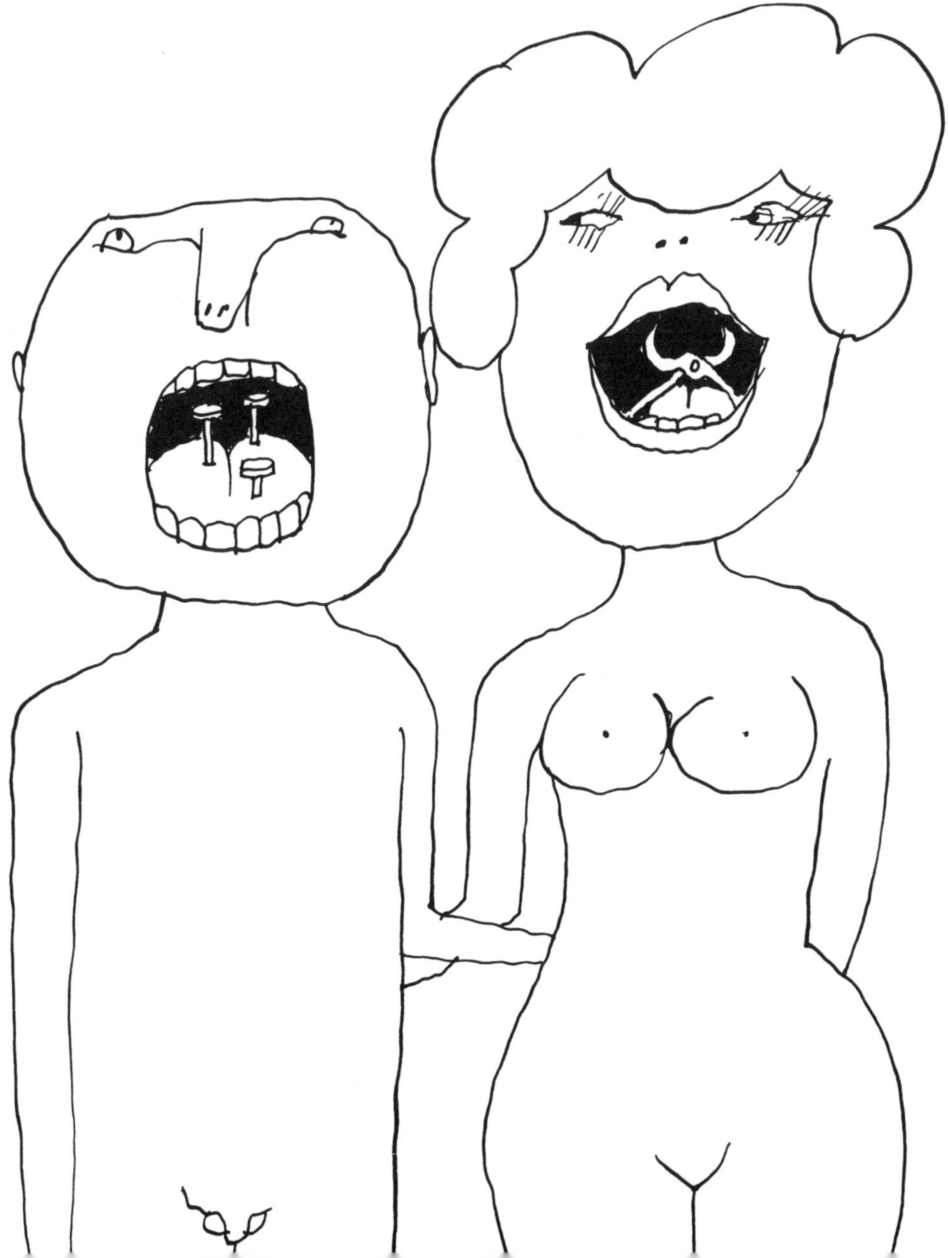

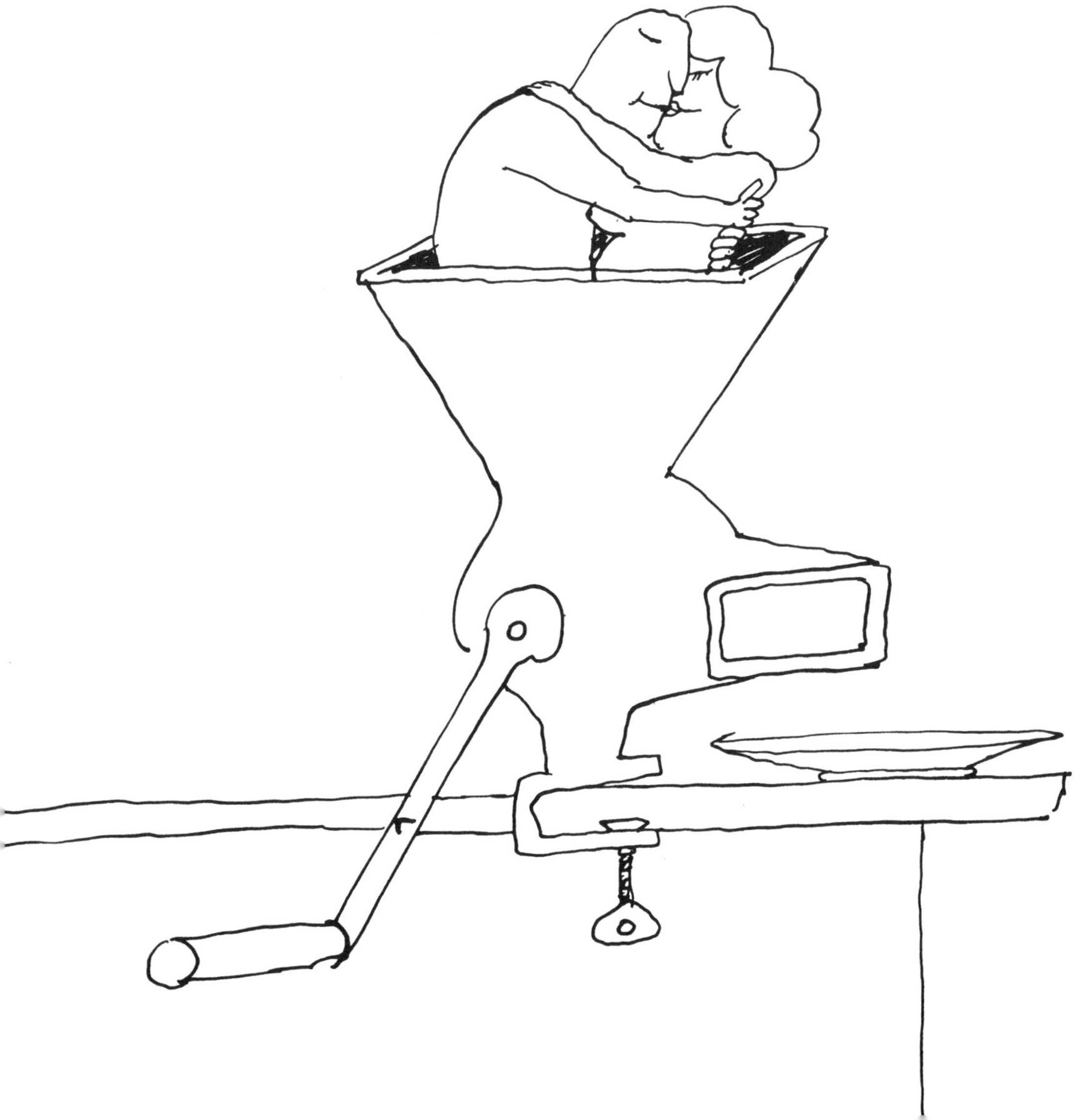

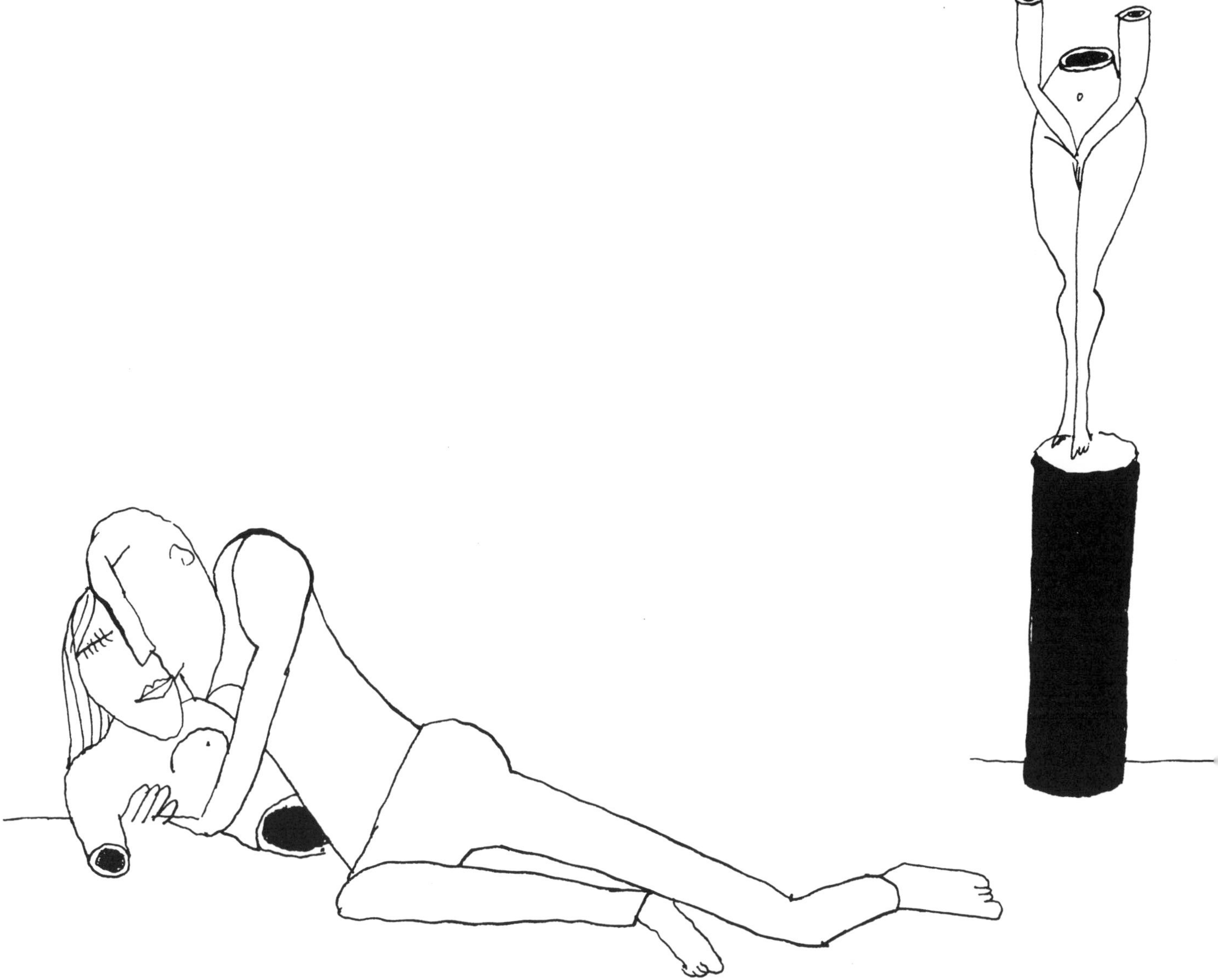

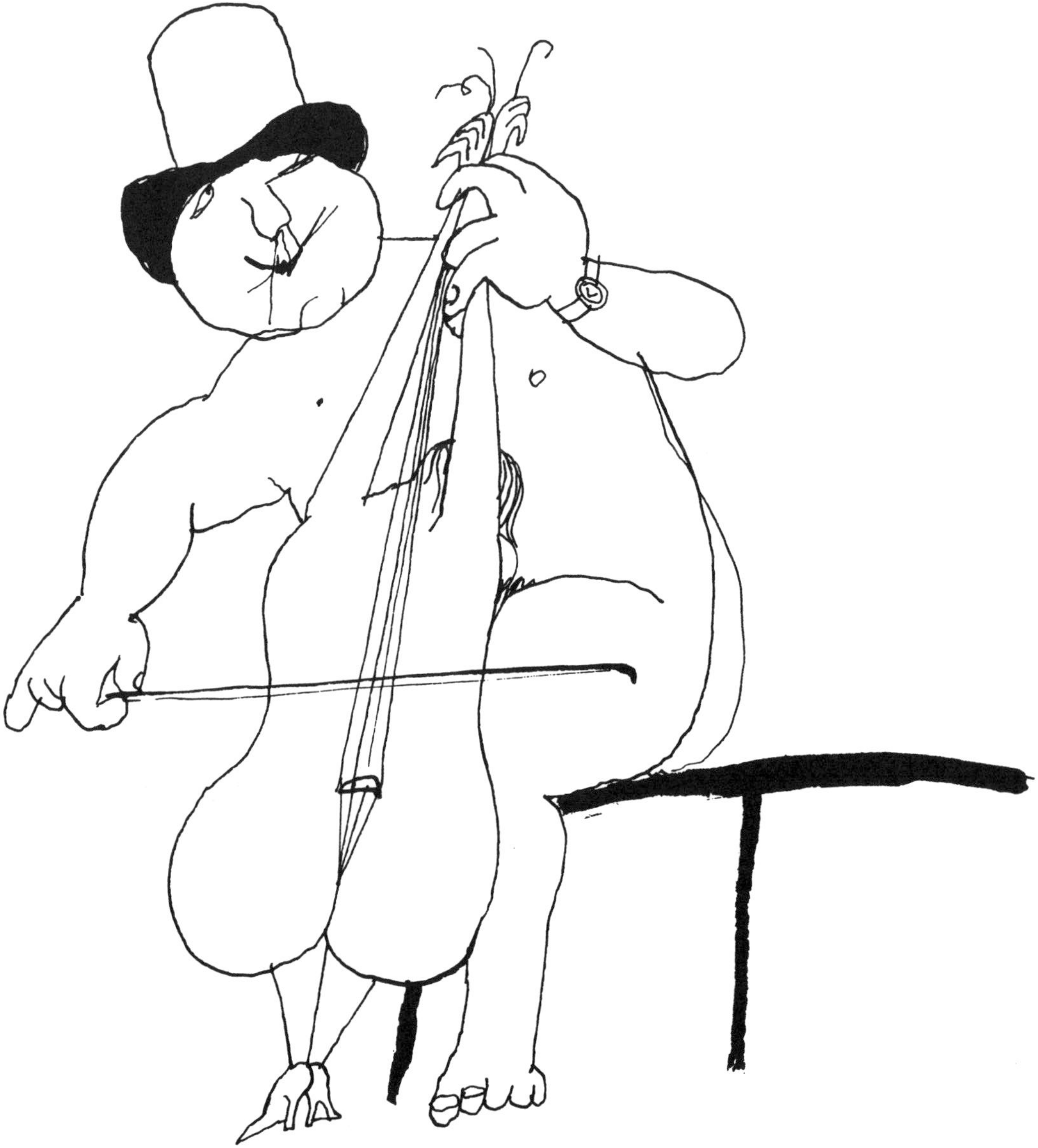

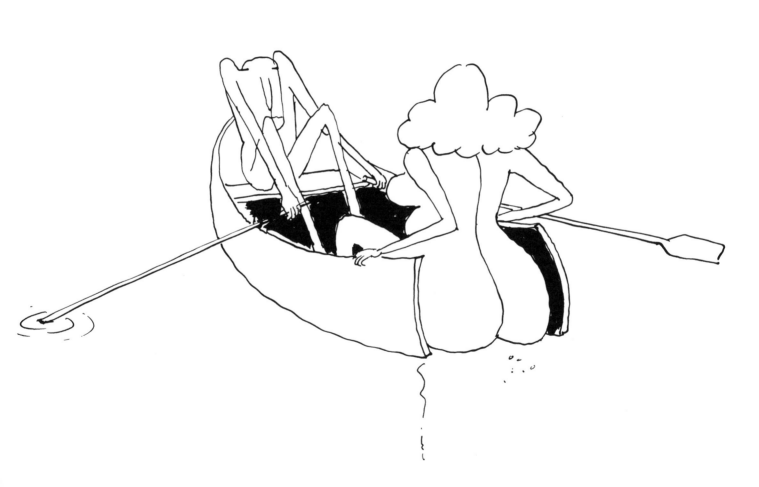

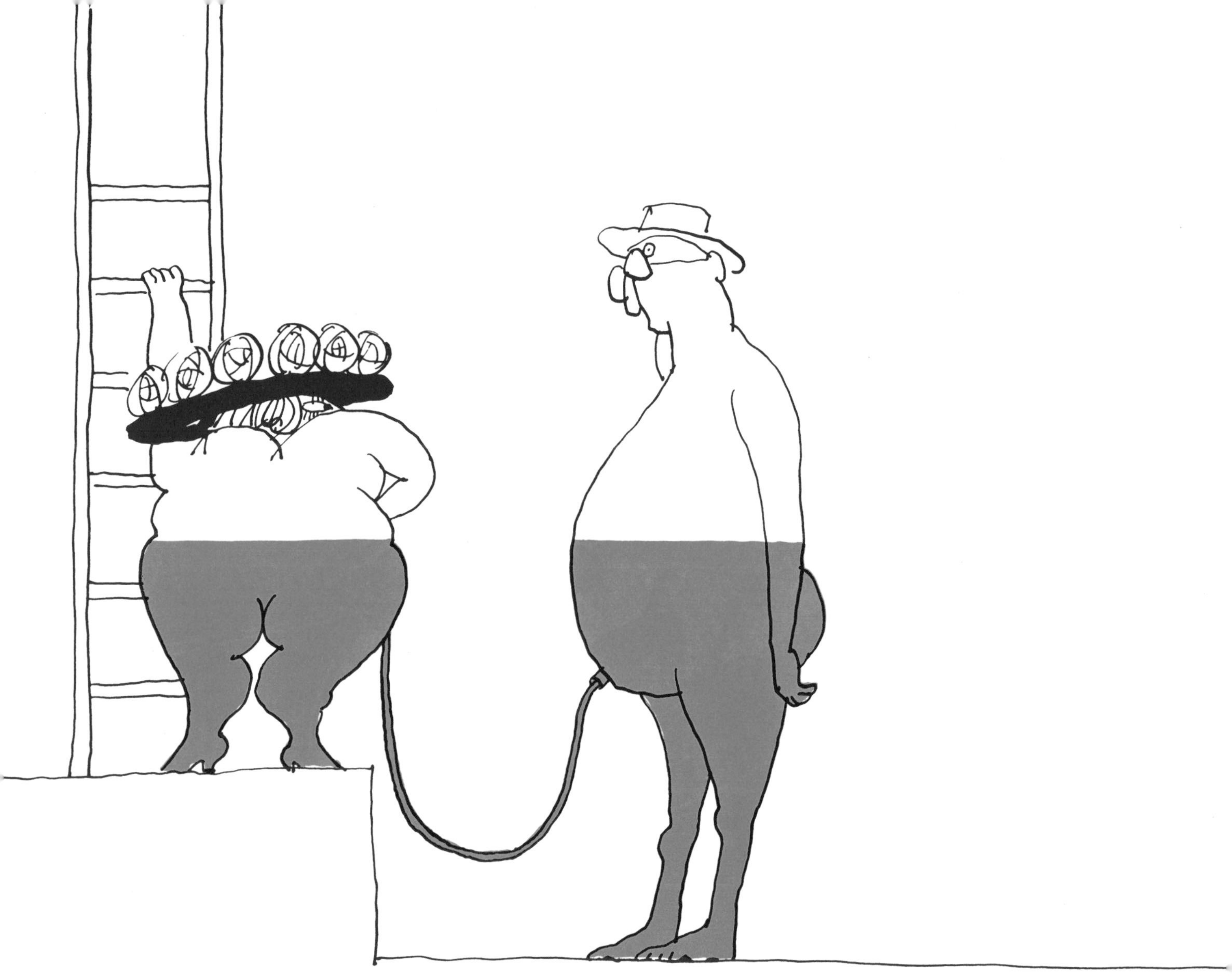

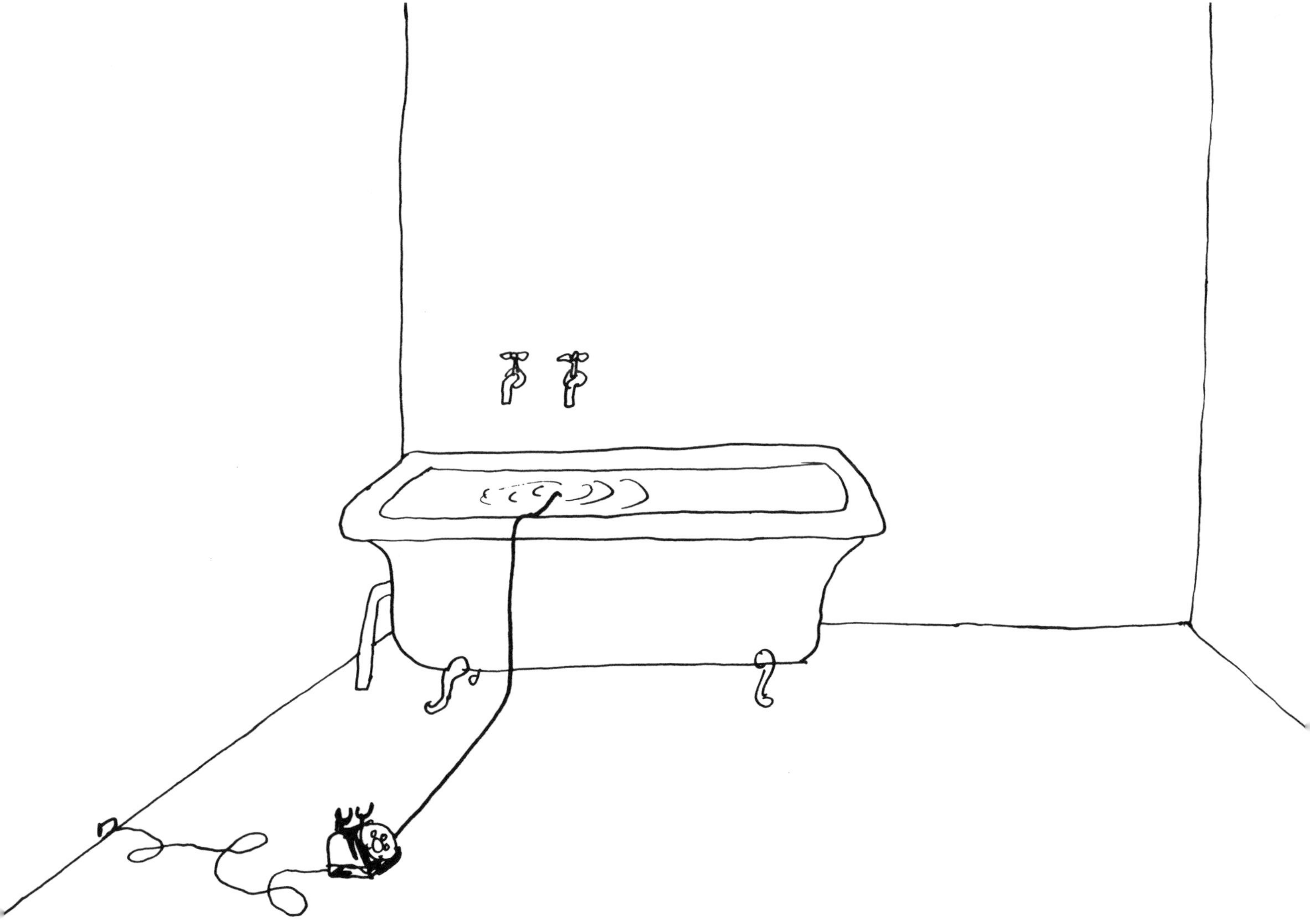

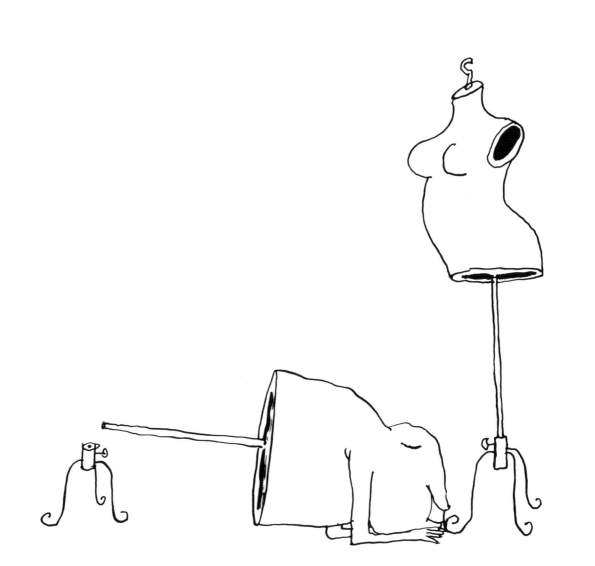

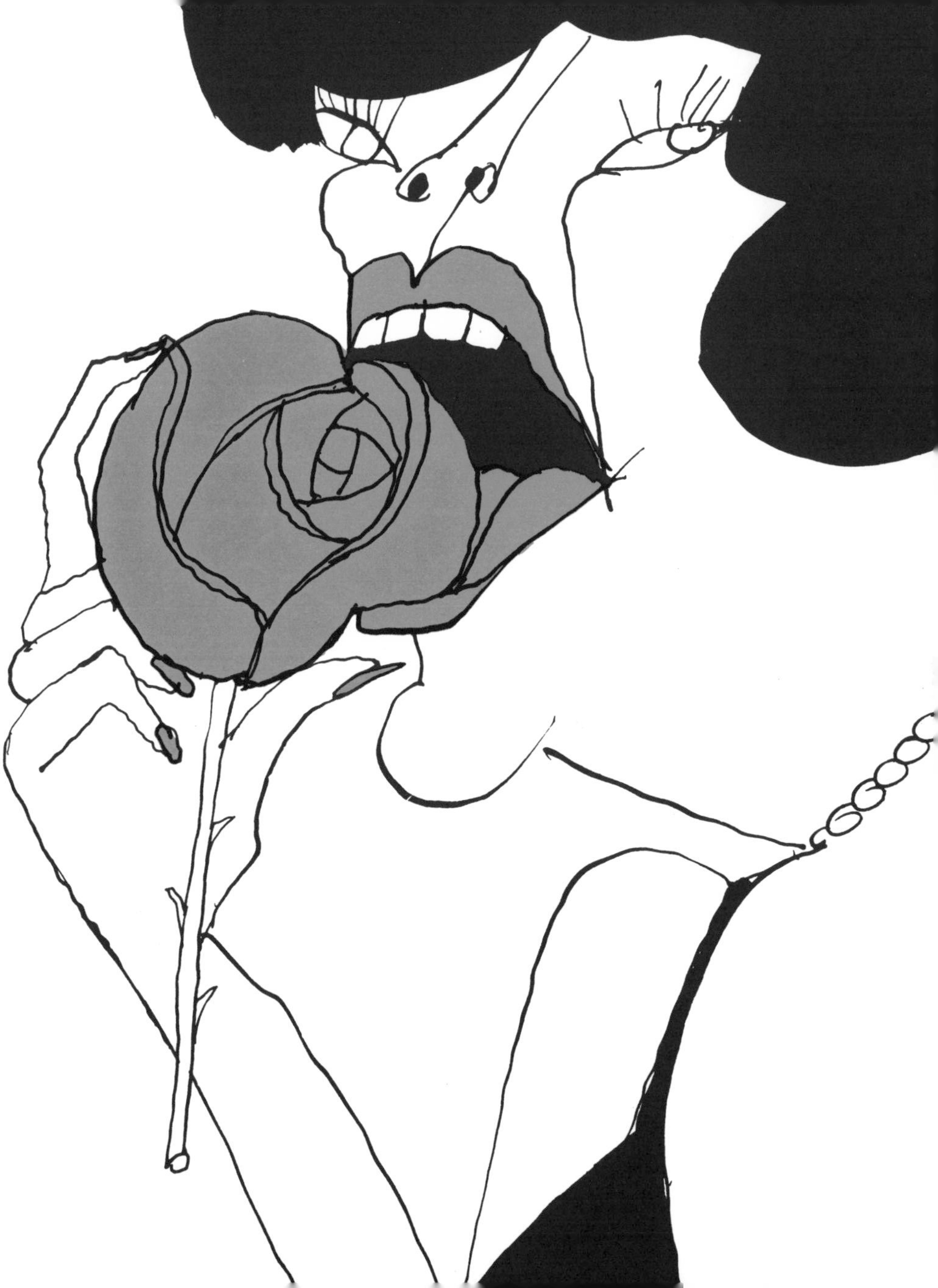

Roseeater

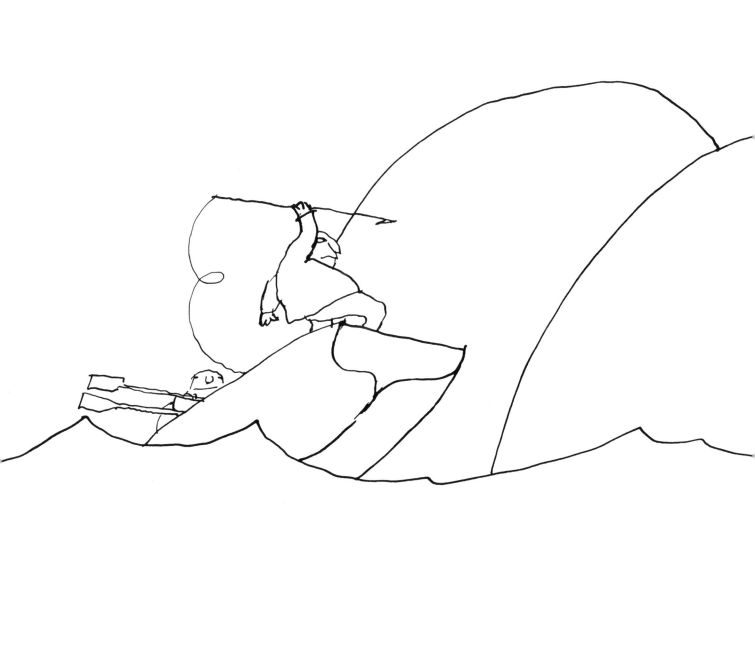

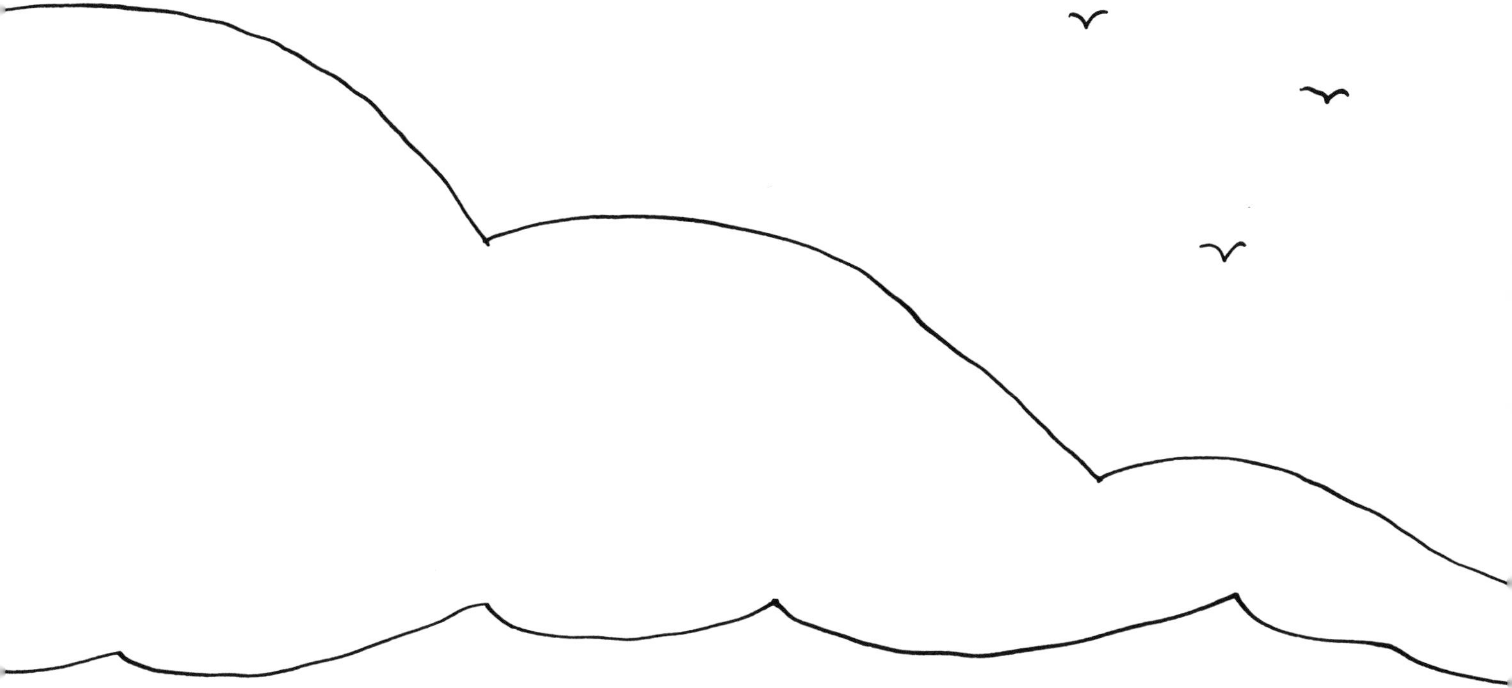

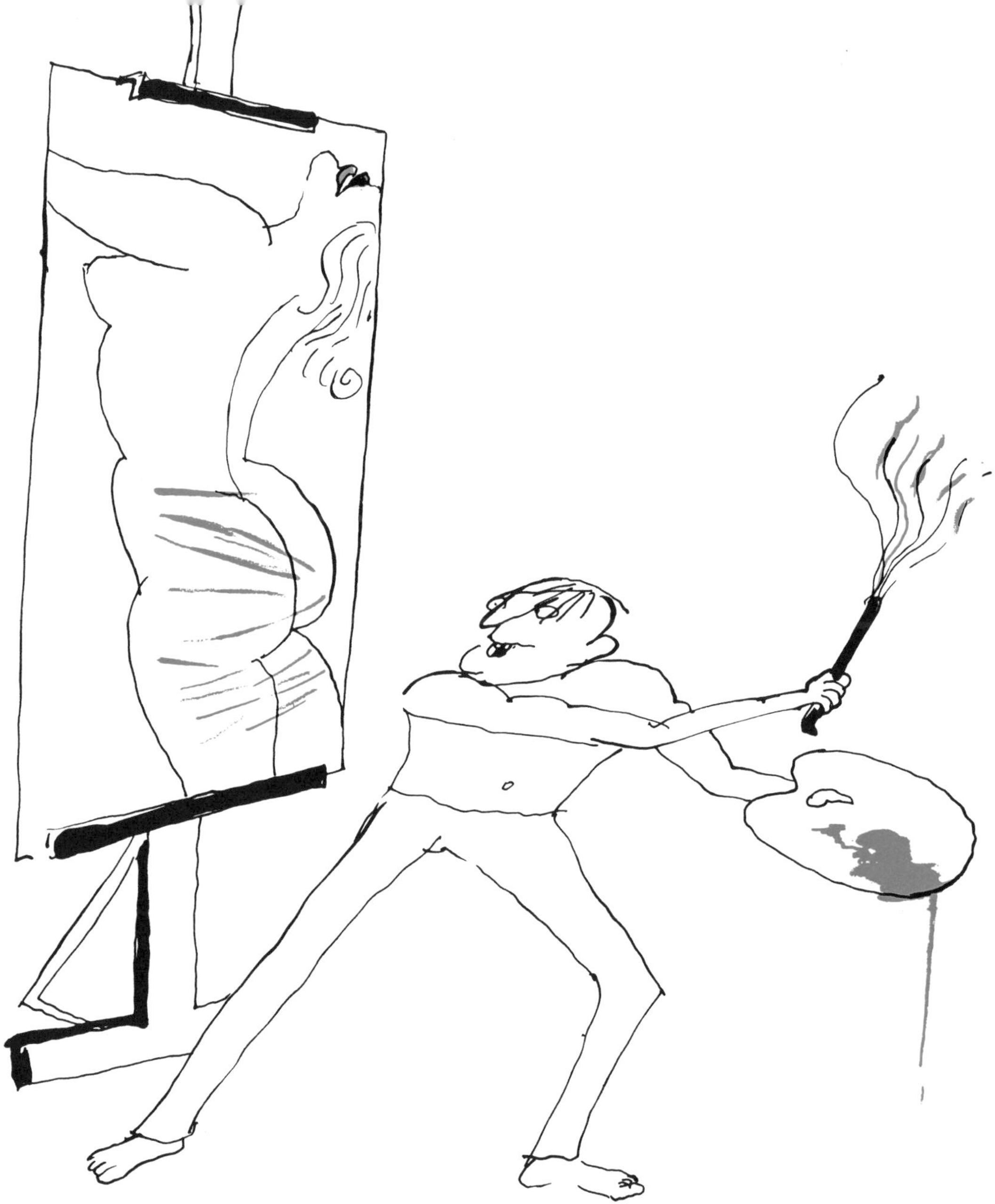

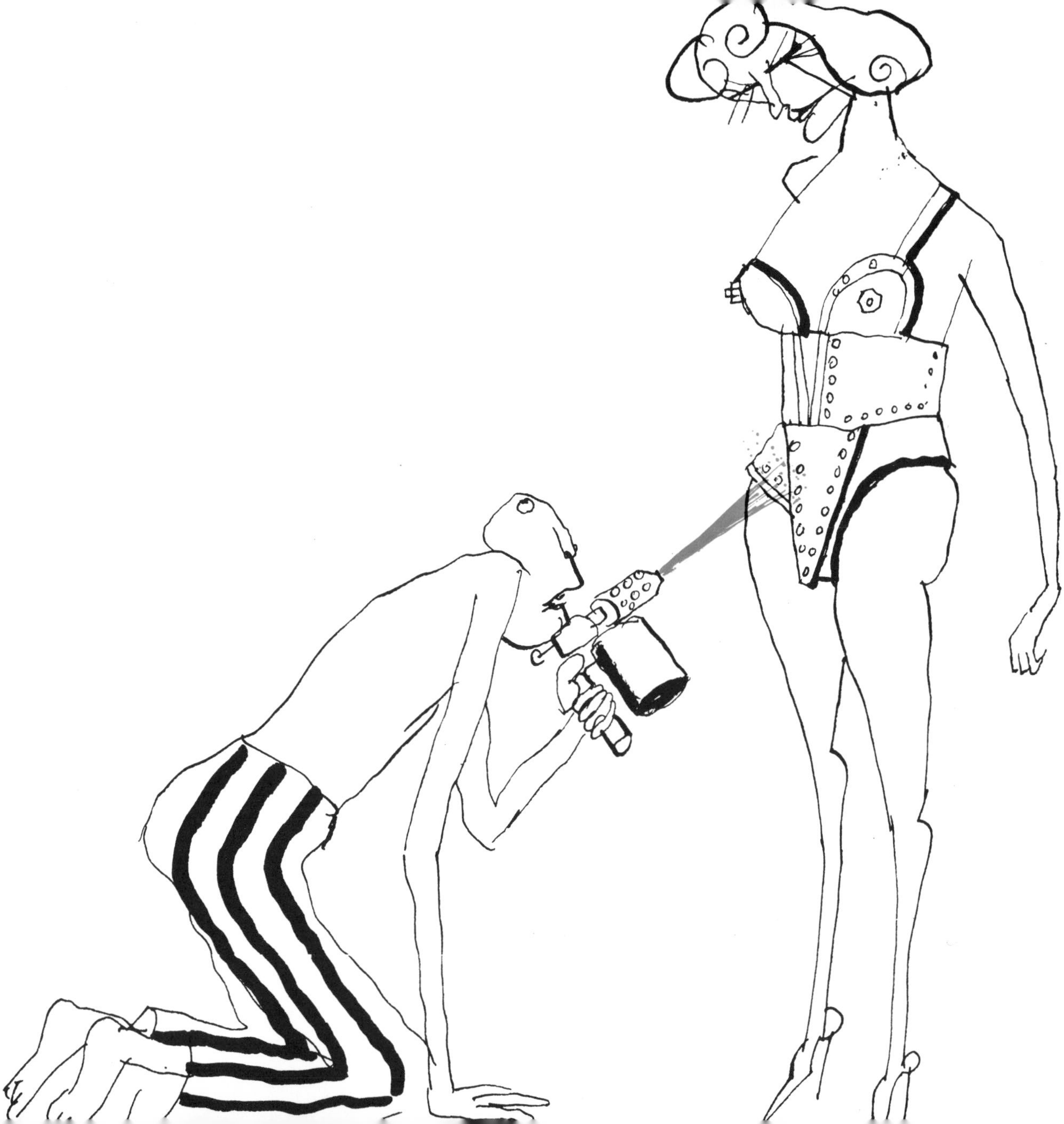

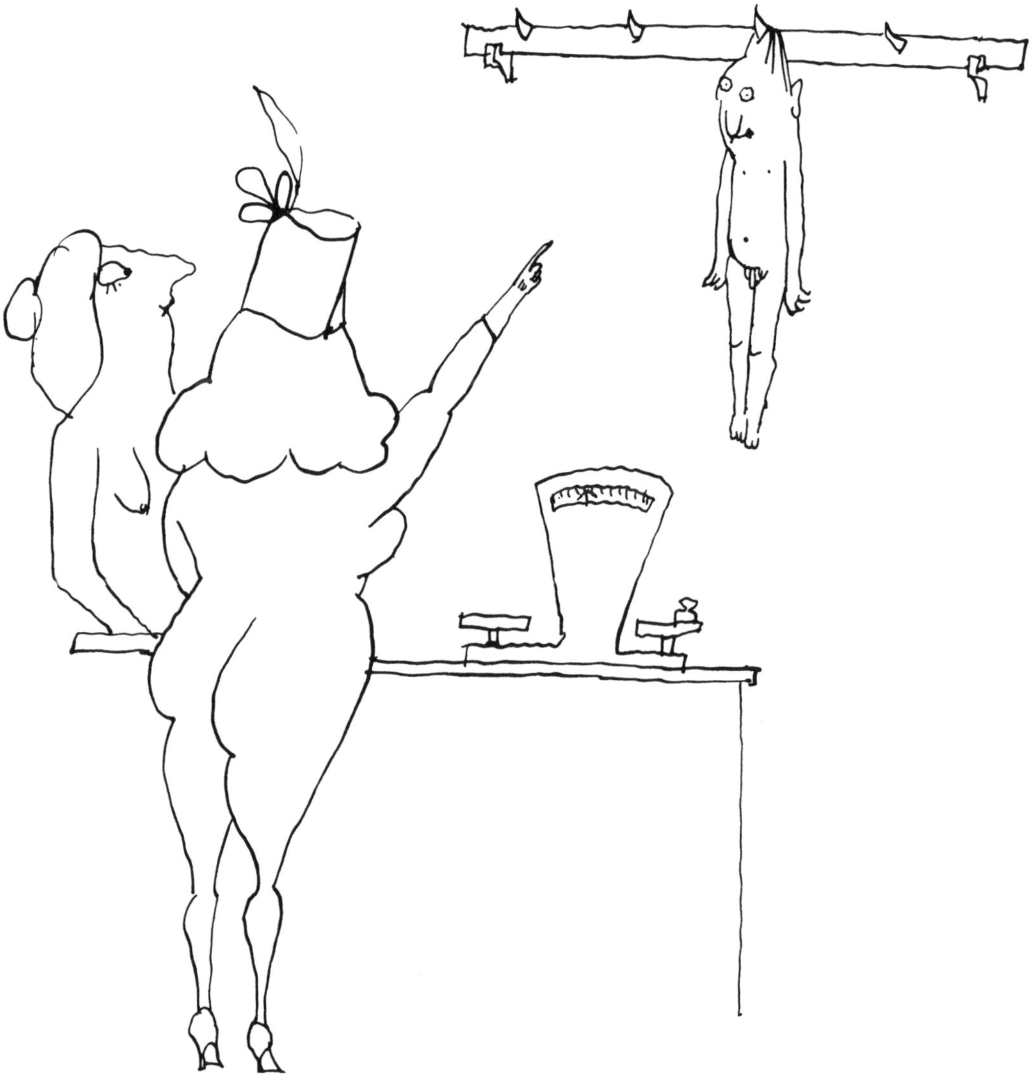

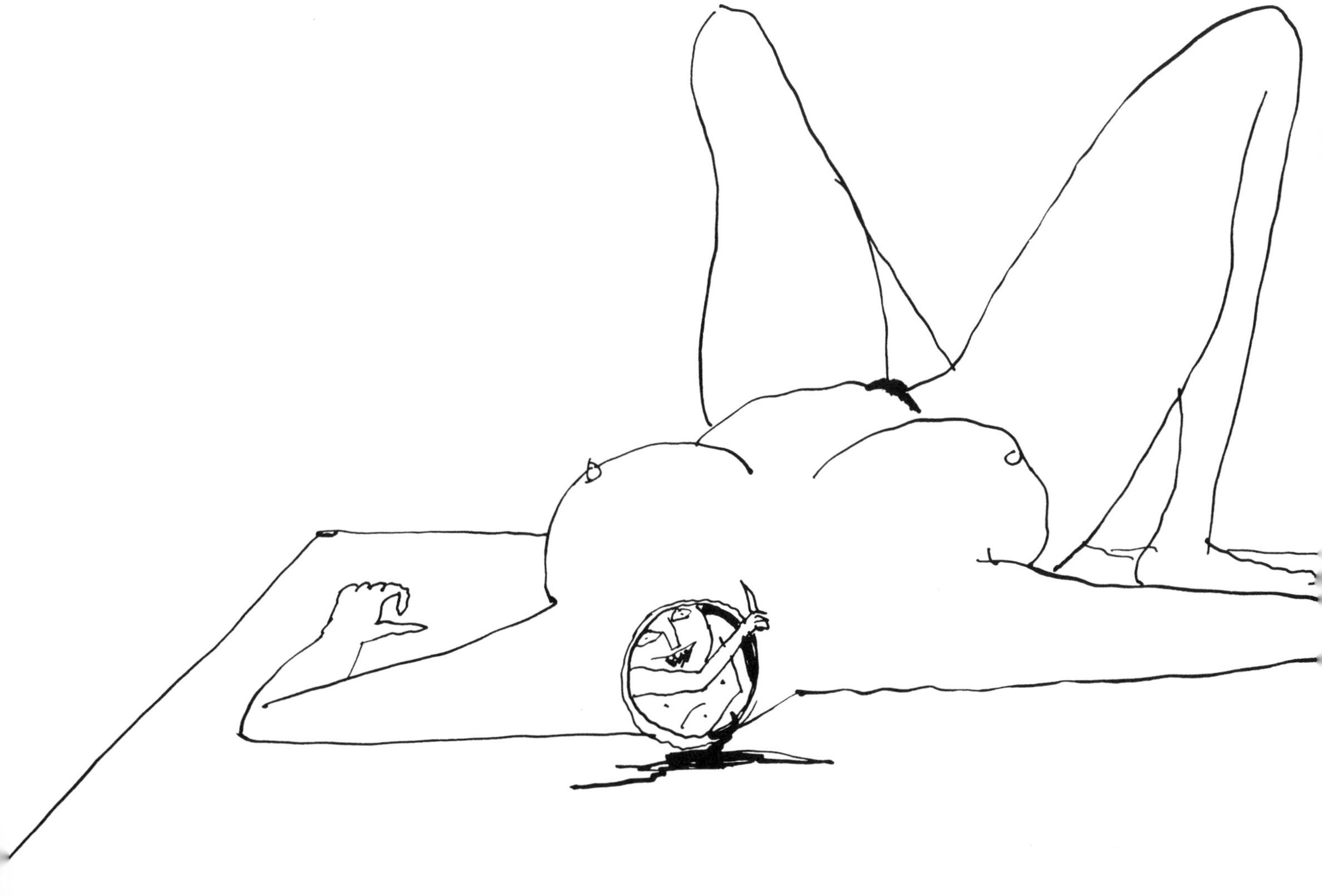

*inventory*

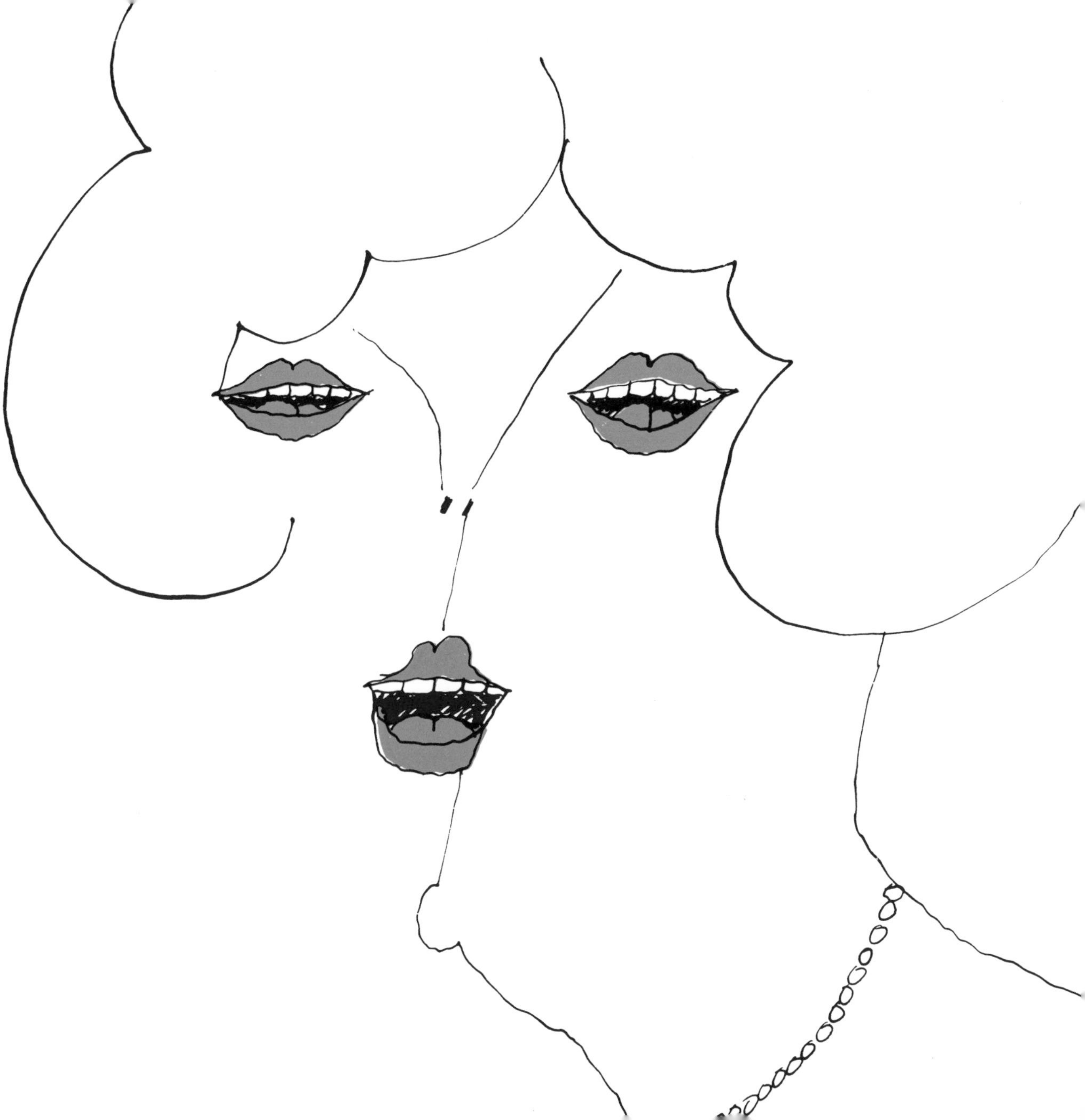

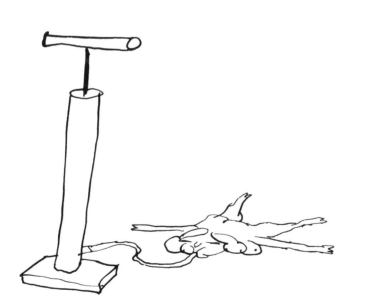

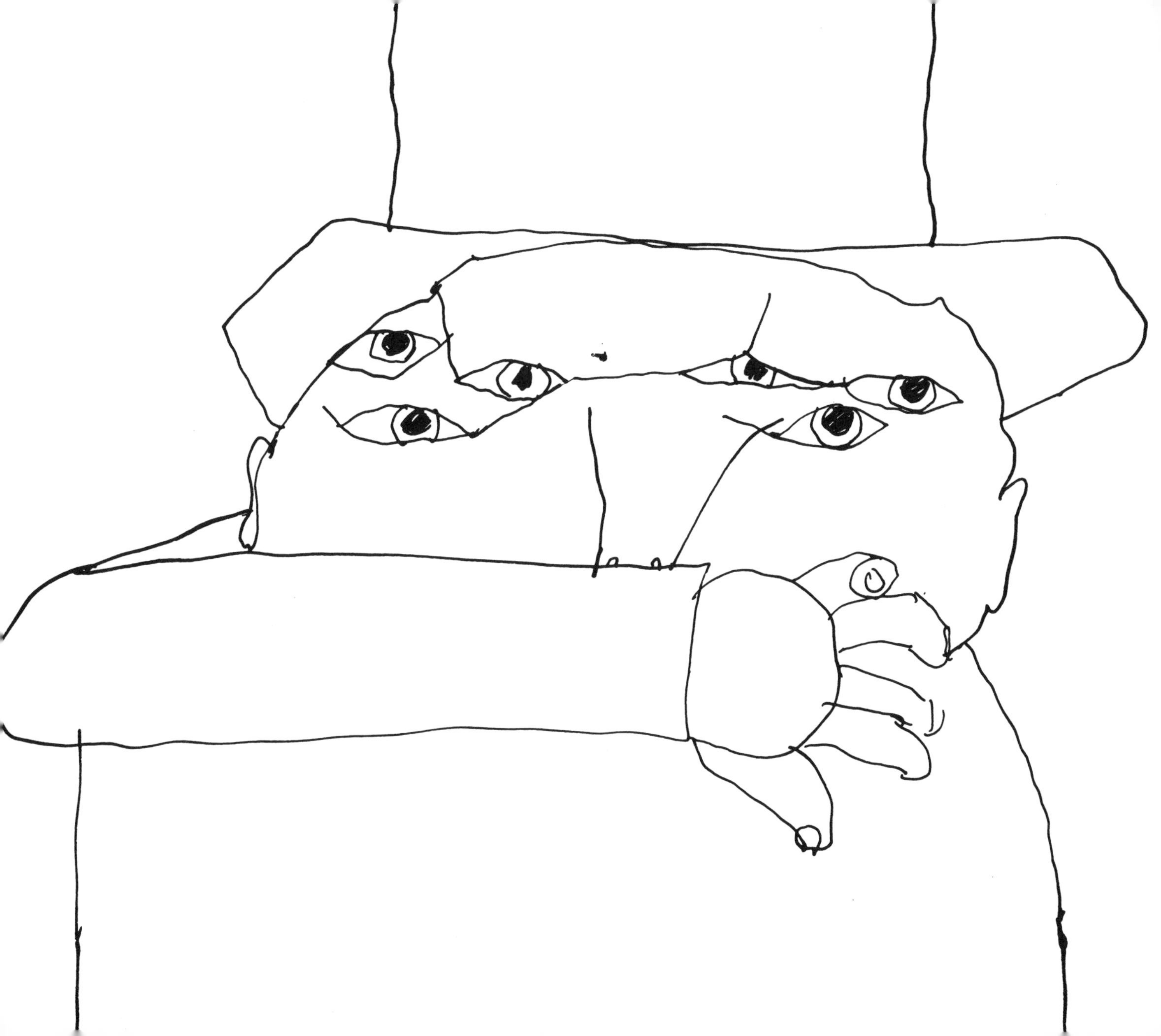

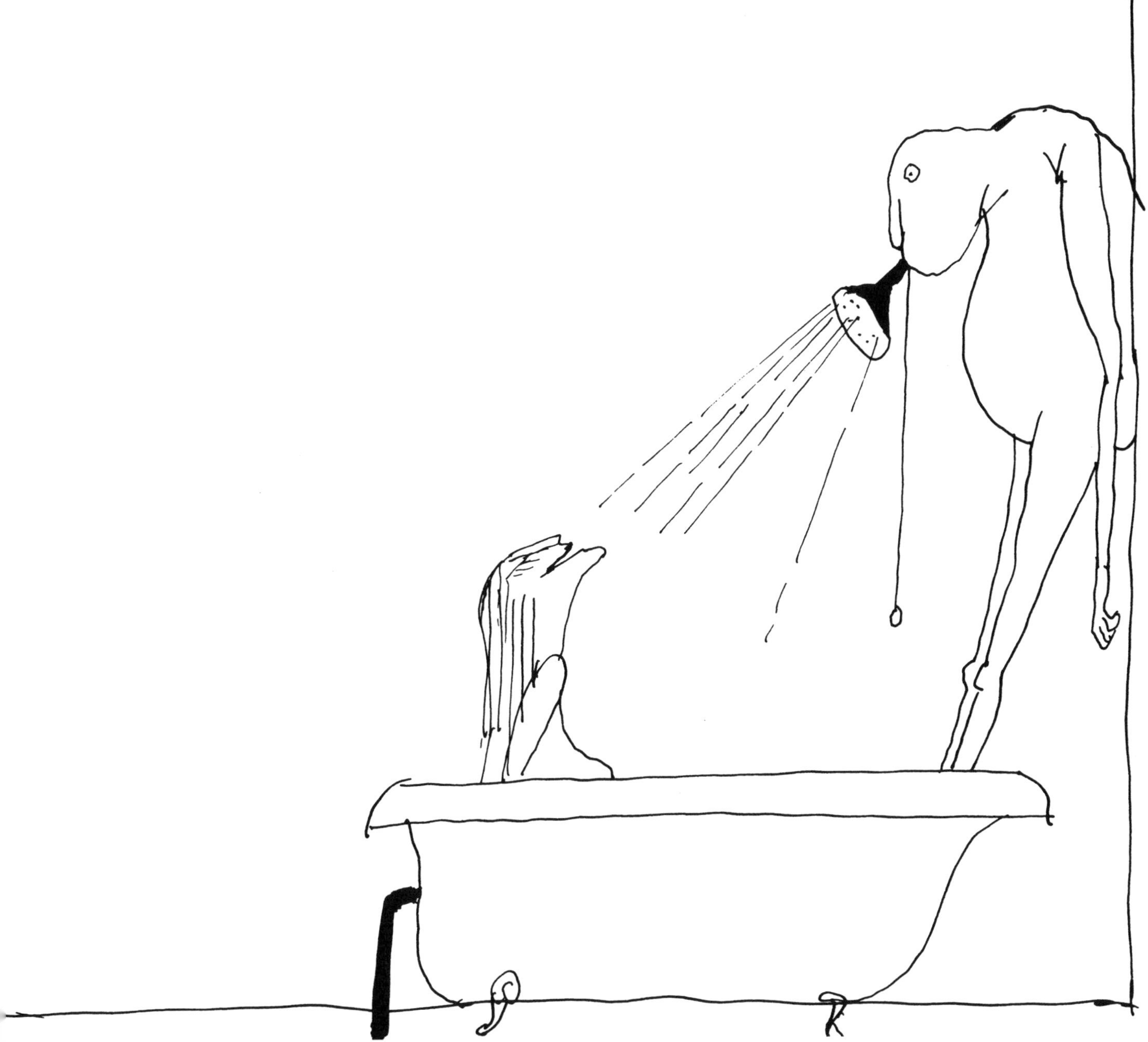

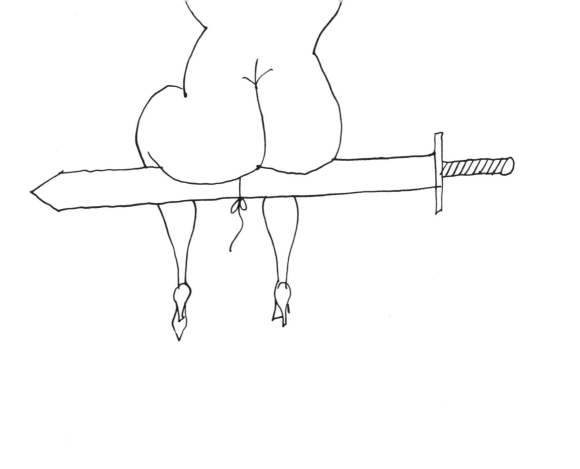

rendez-vous

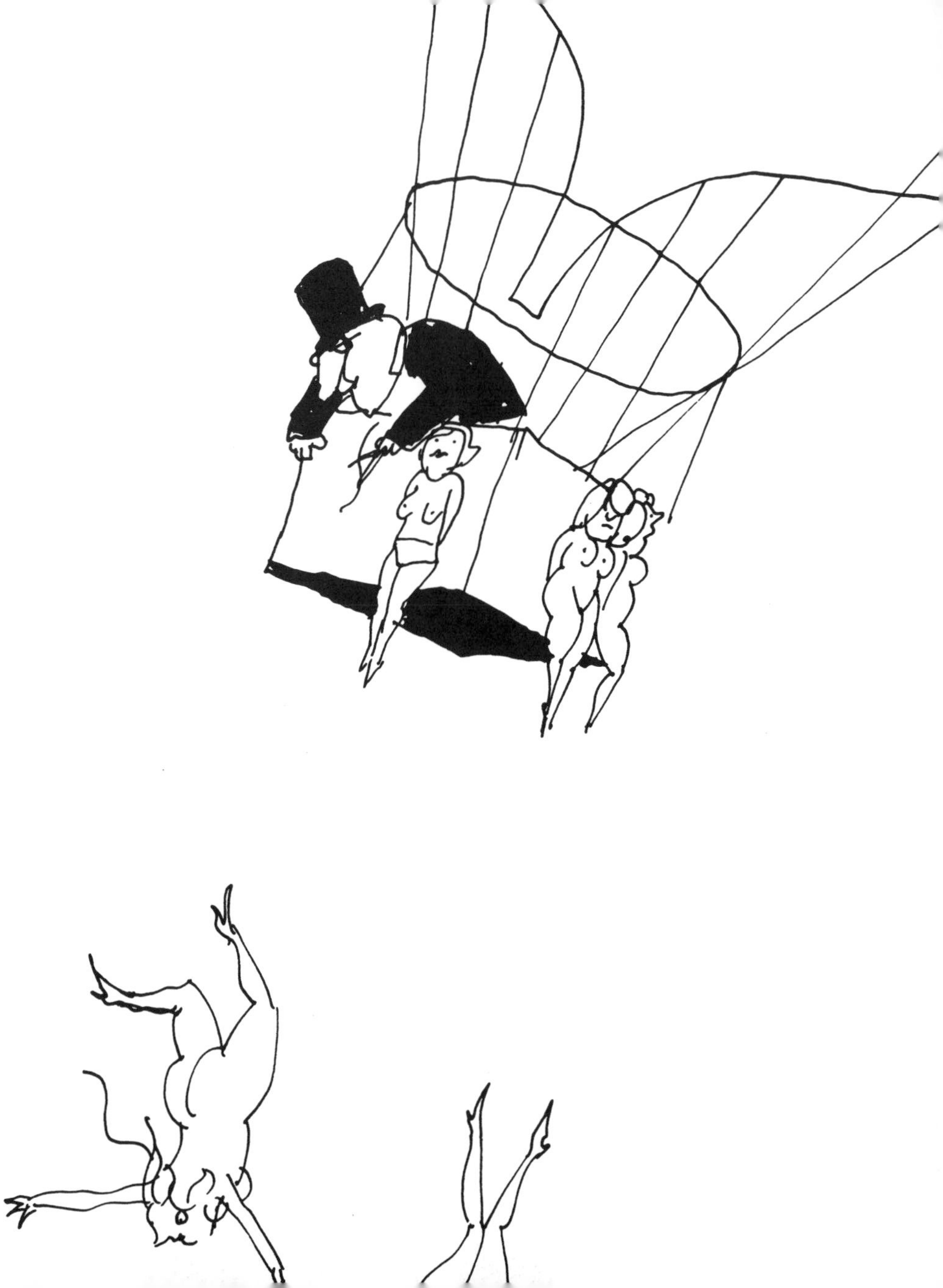

Ballast

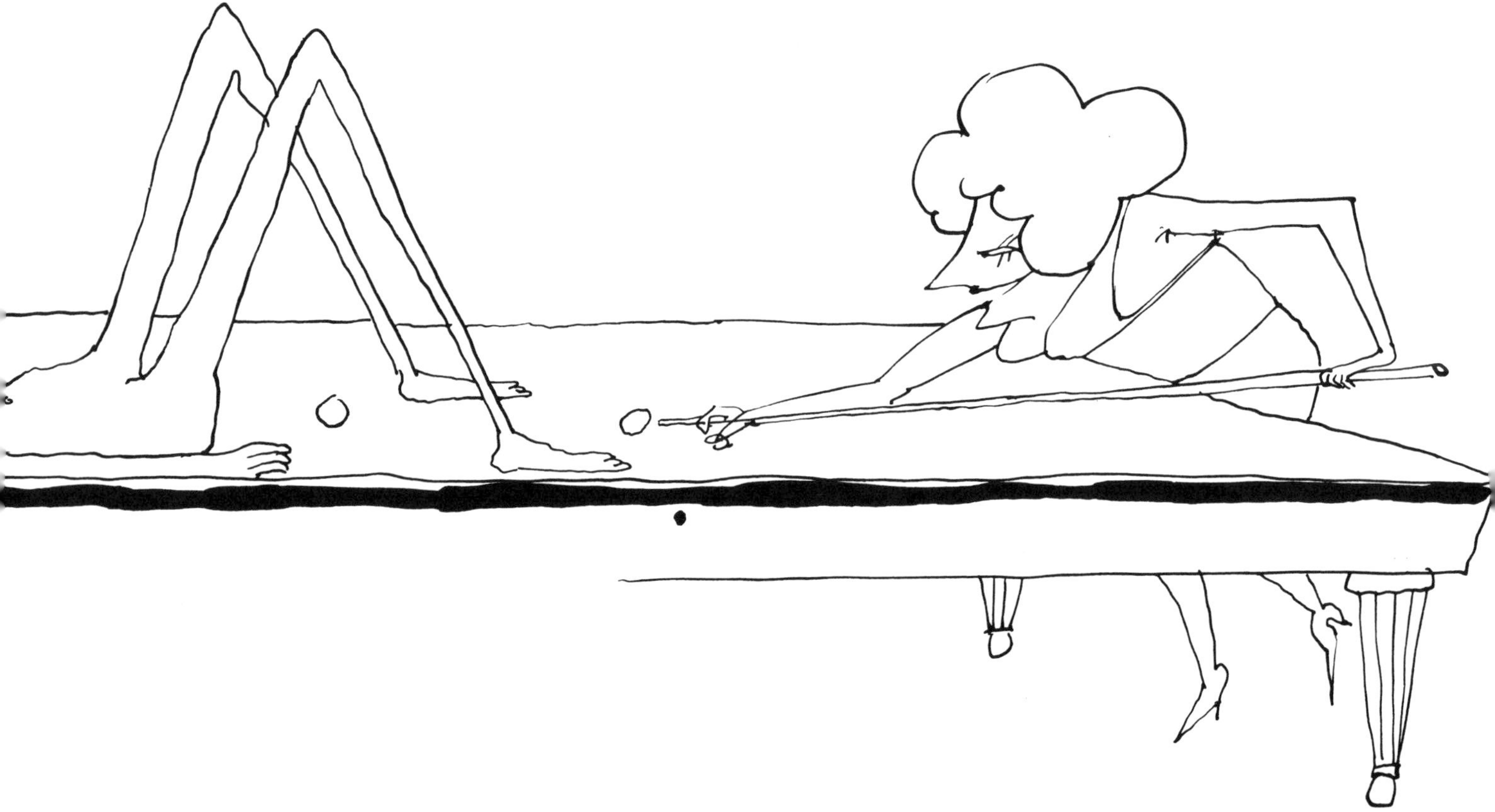

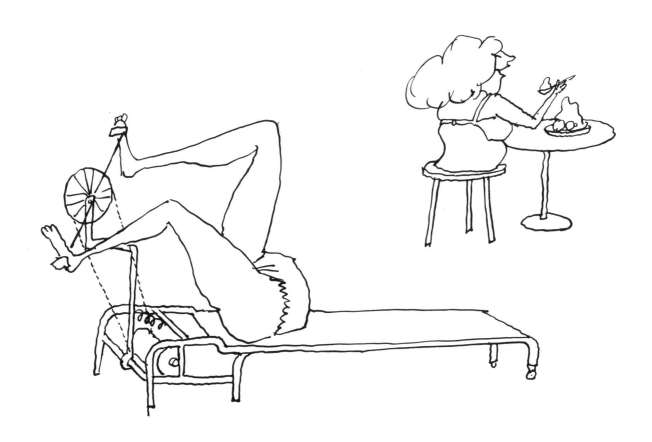

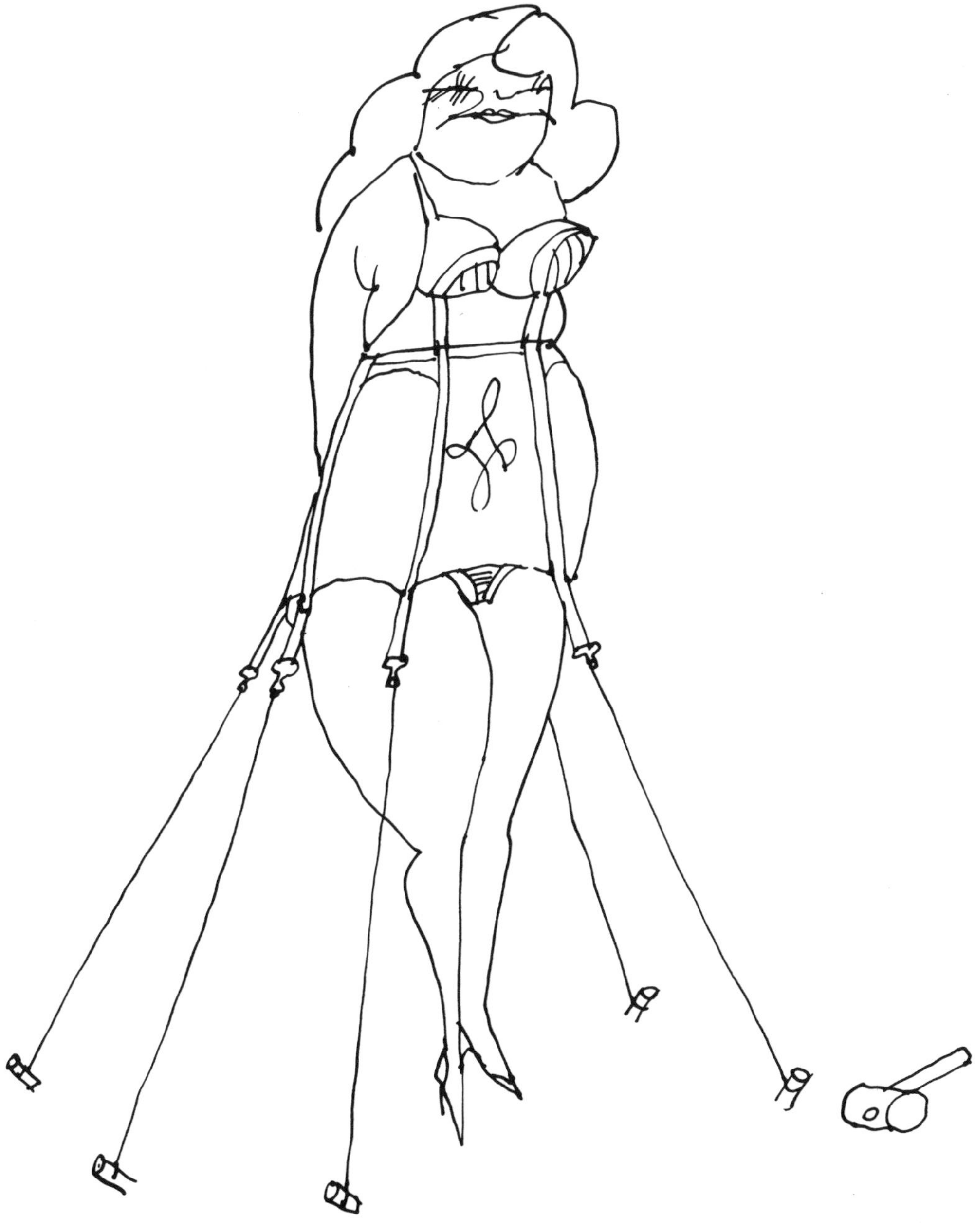

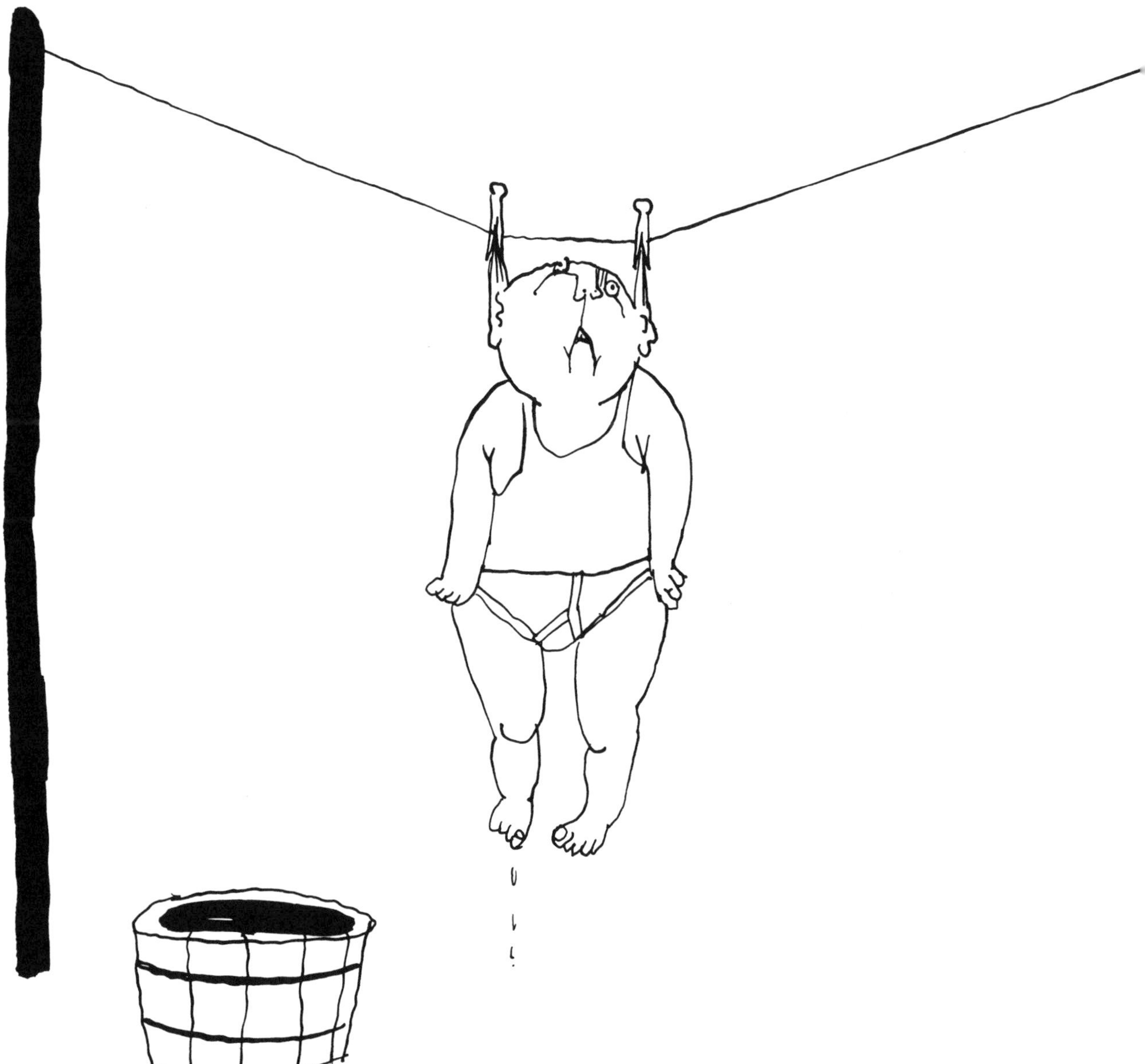

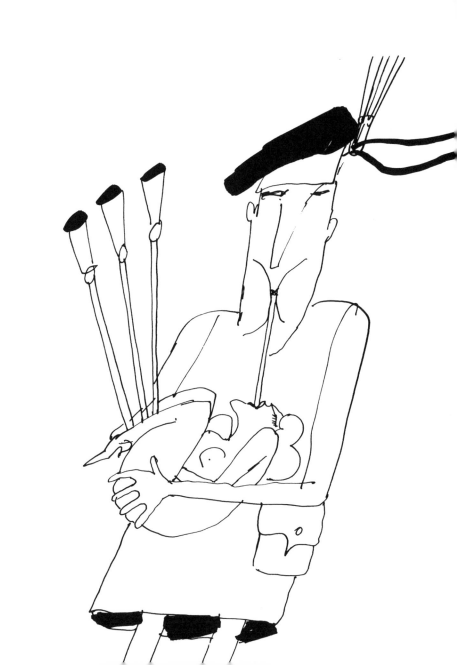

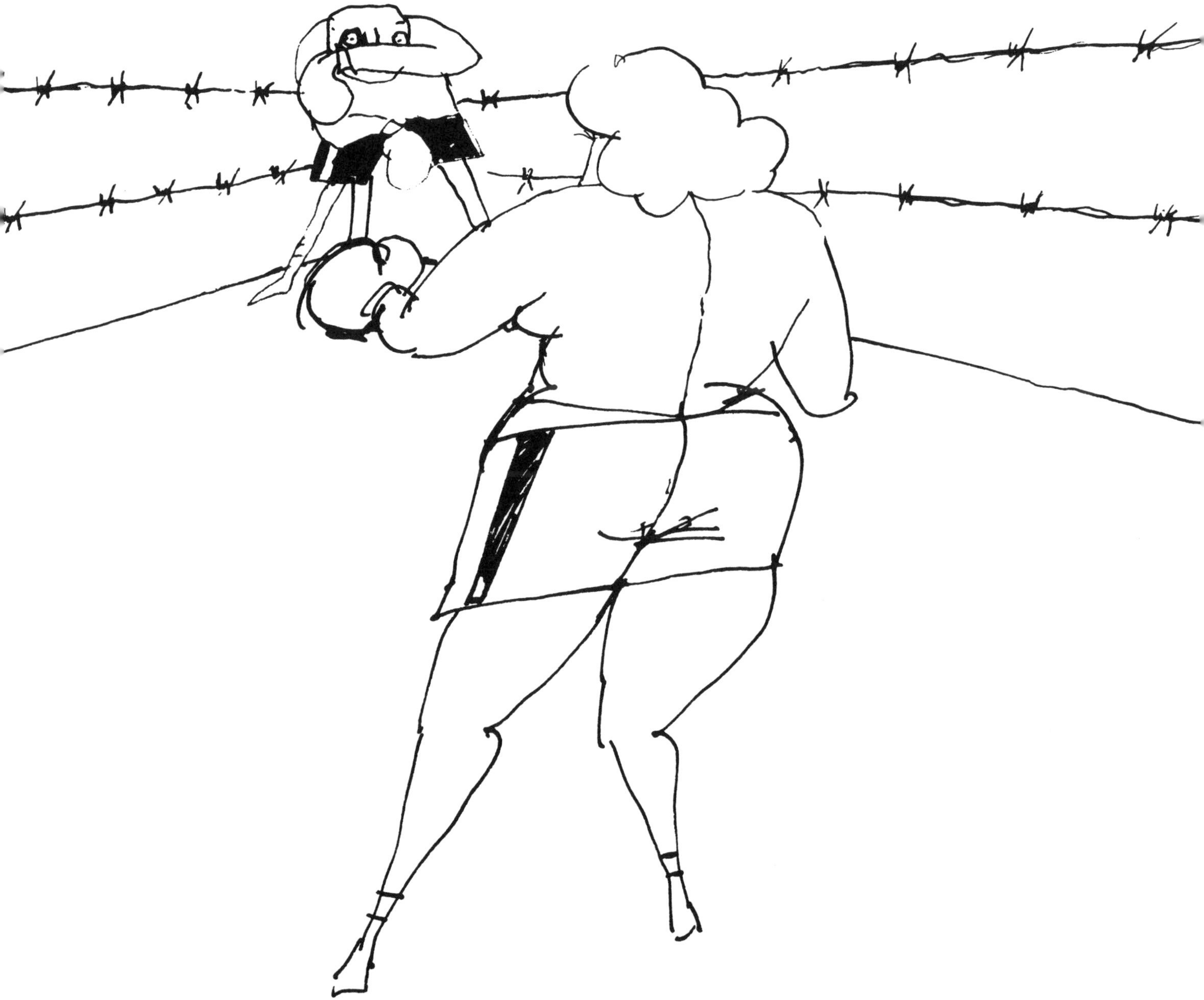

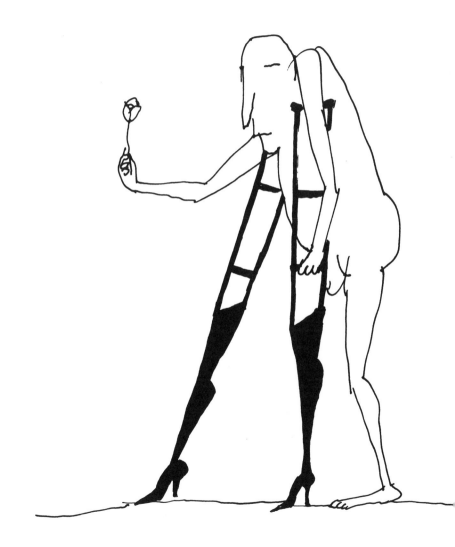

memories

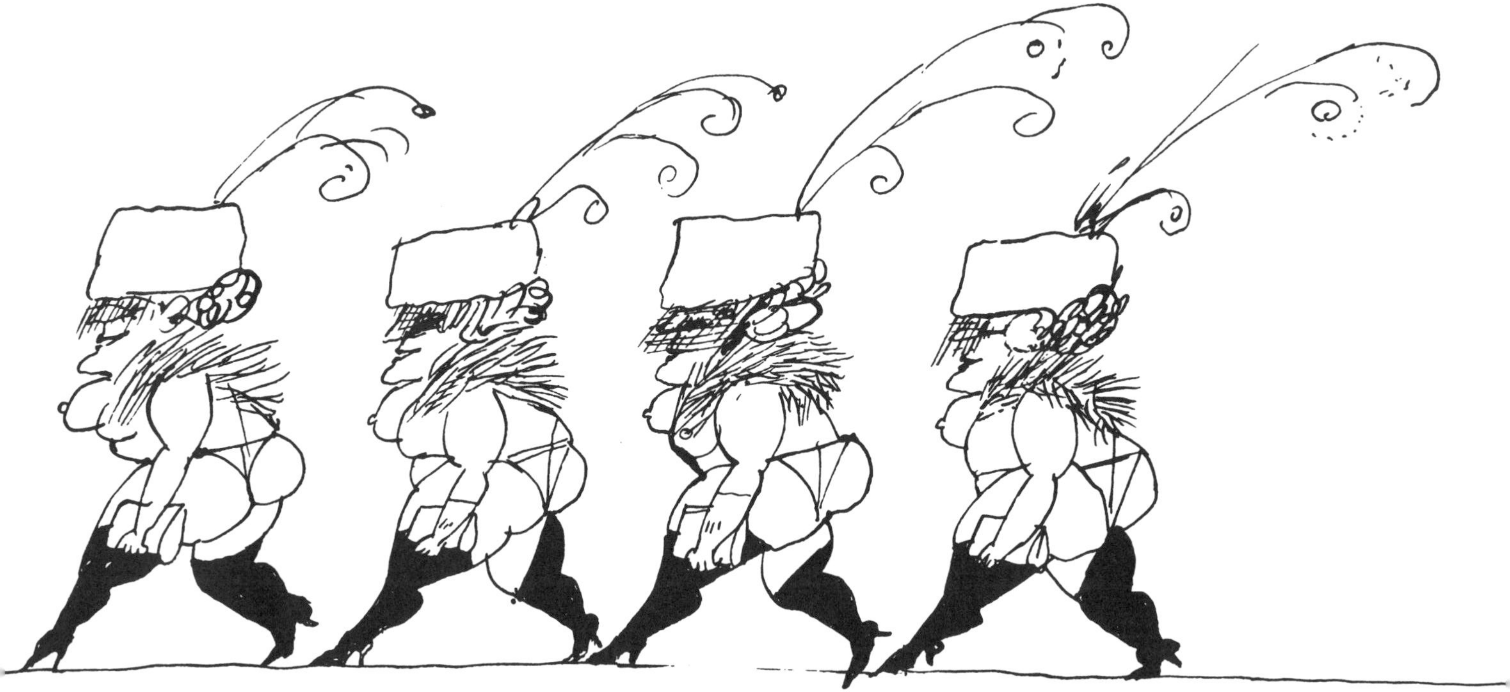

the choice

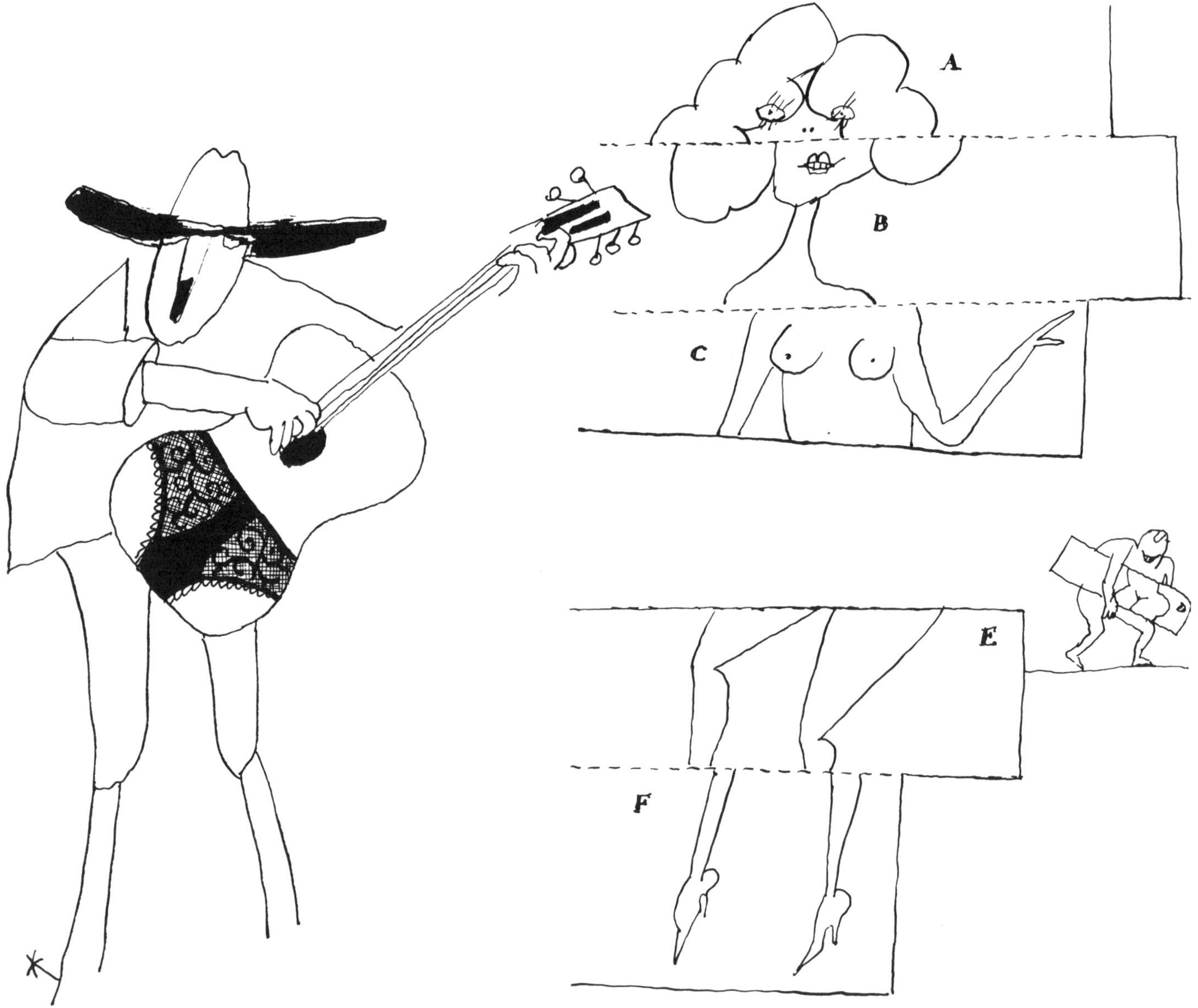
A
B
C
D
E
F

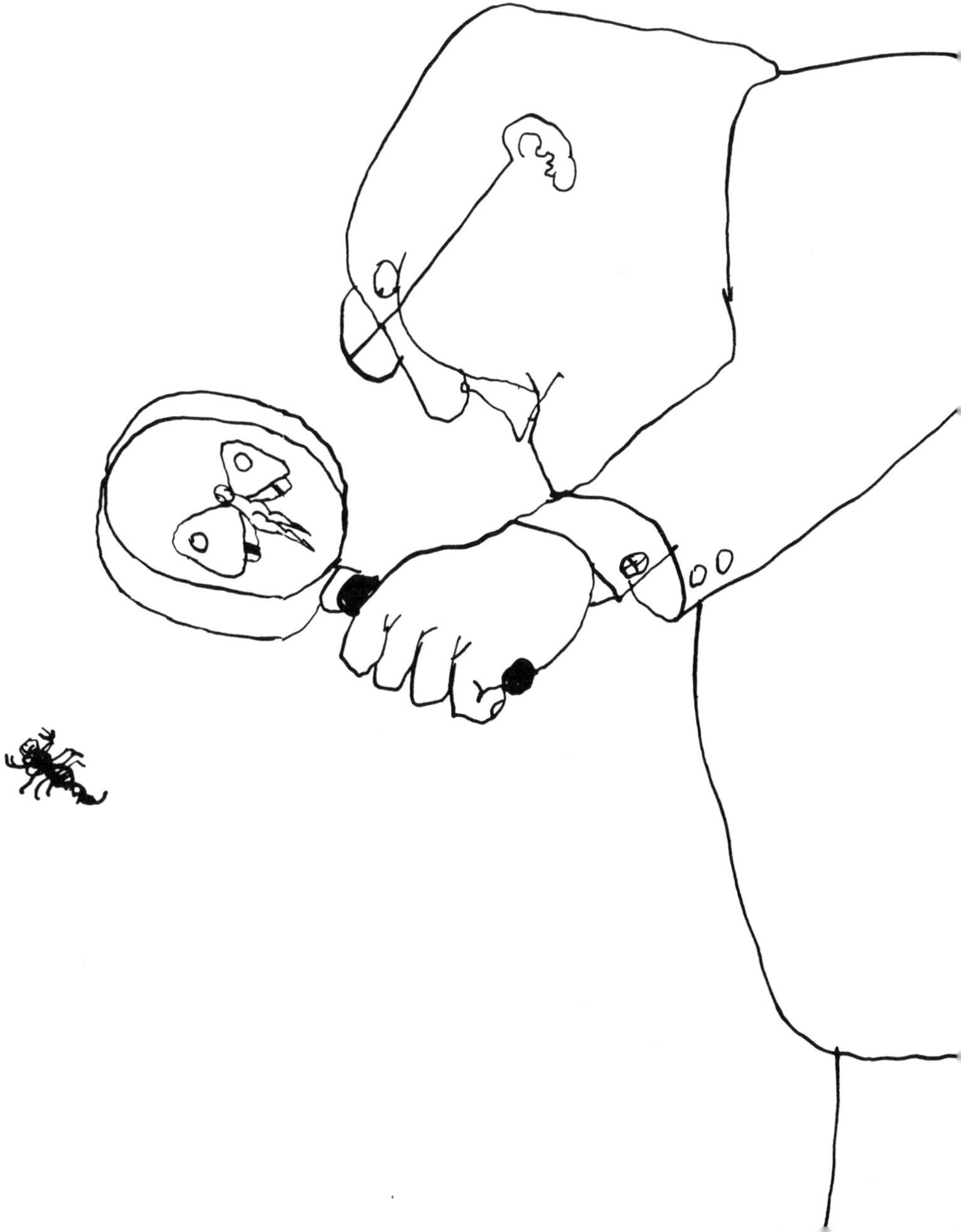

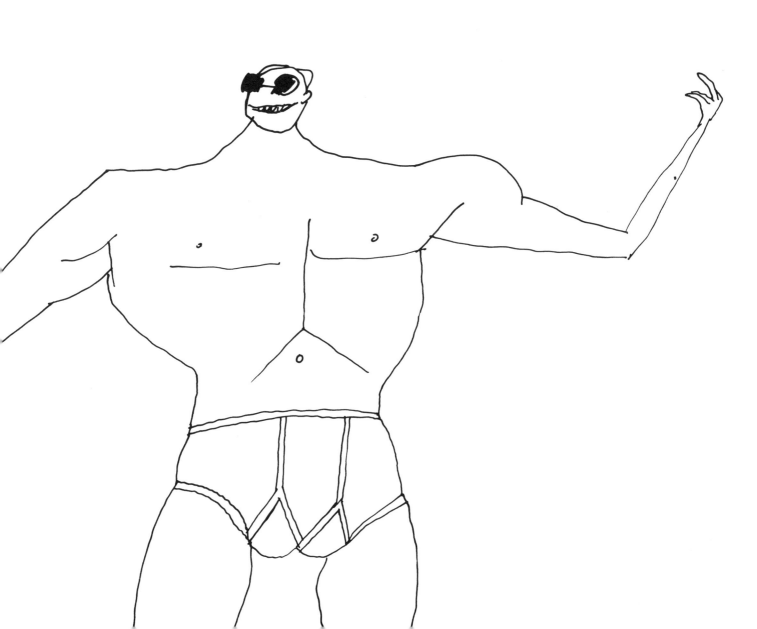

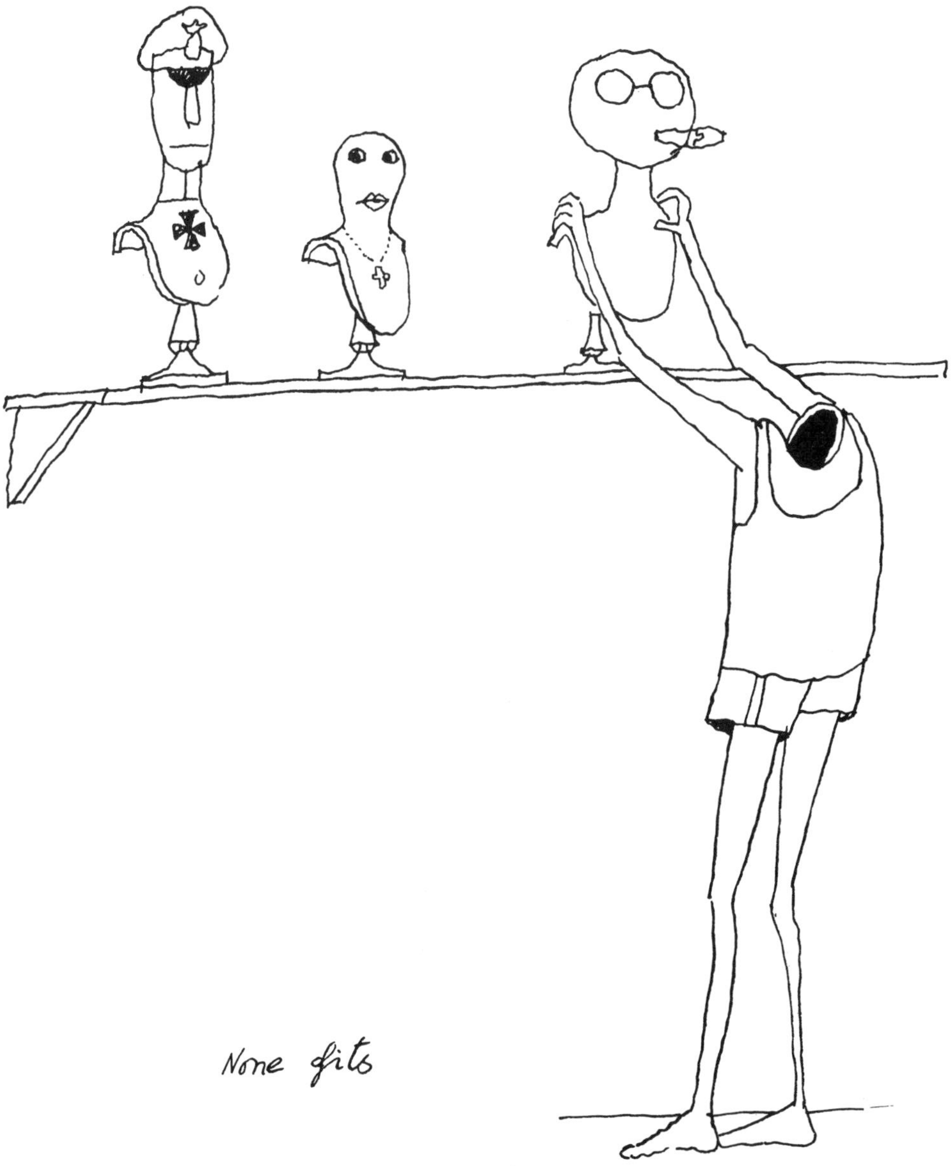

None fits

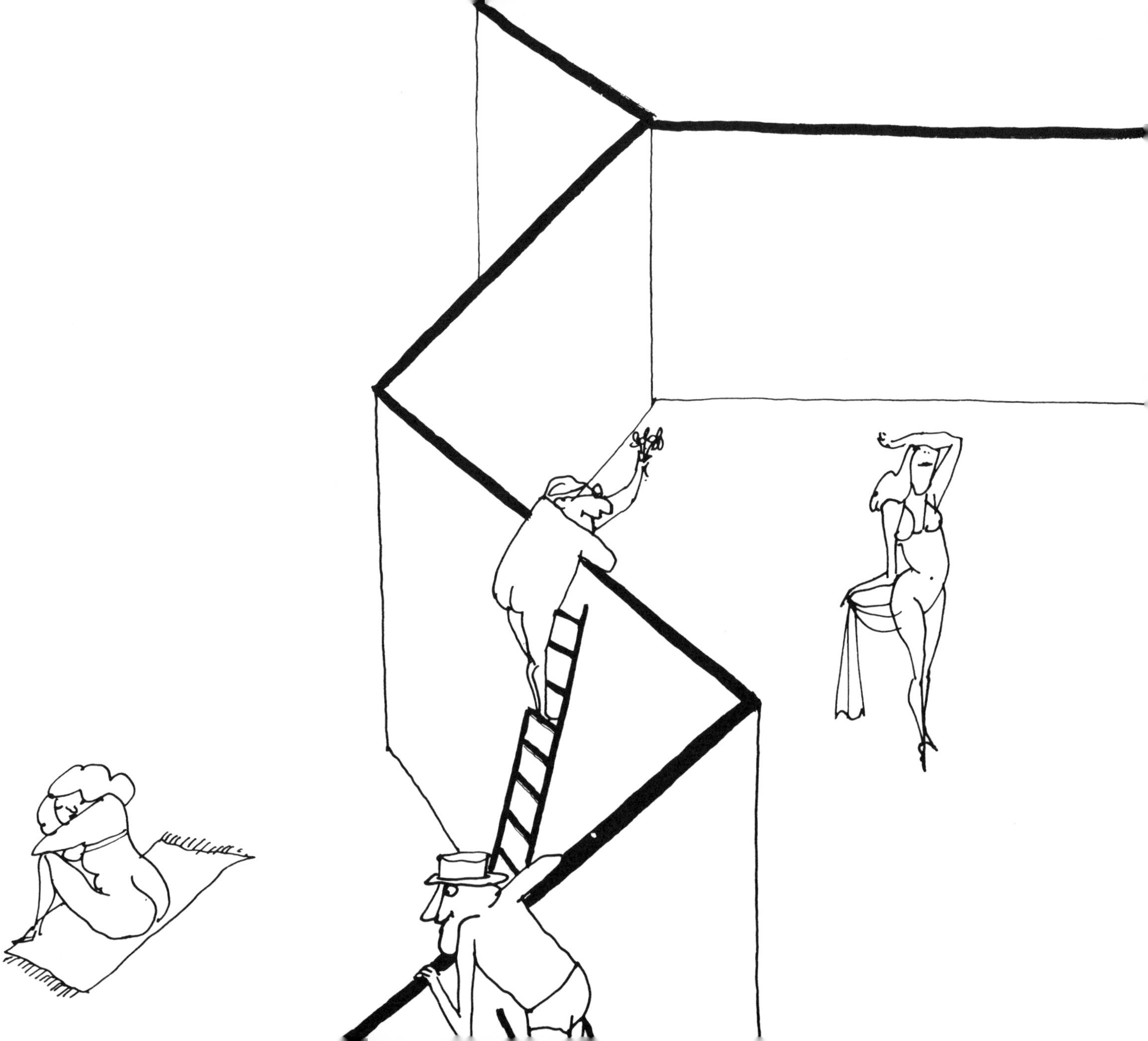

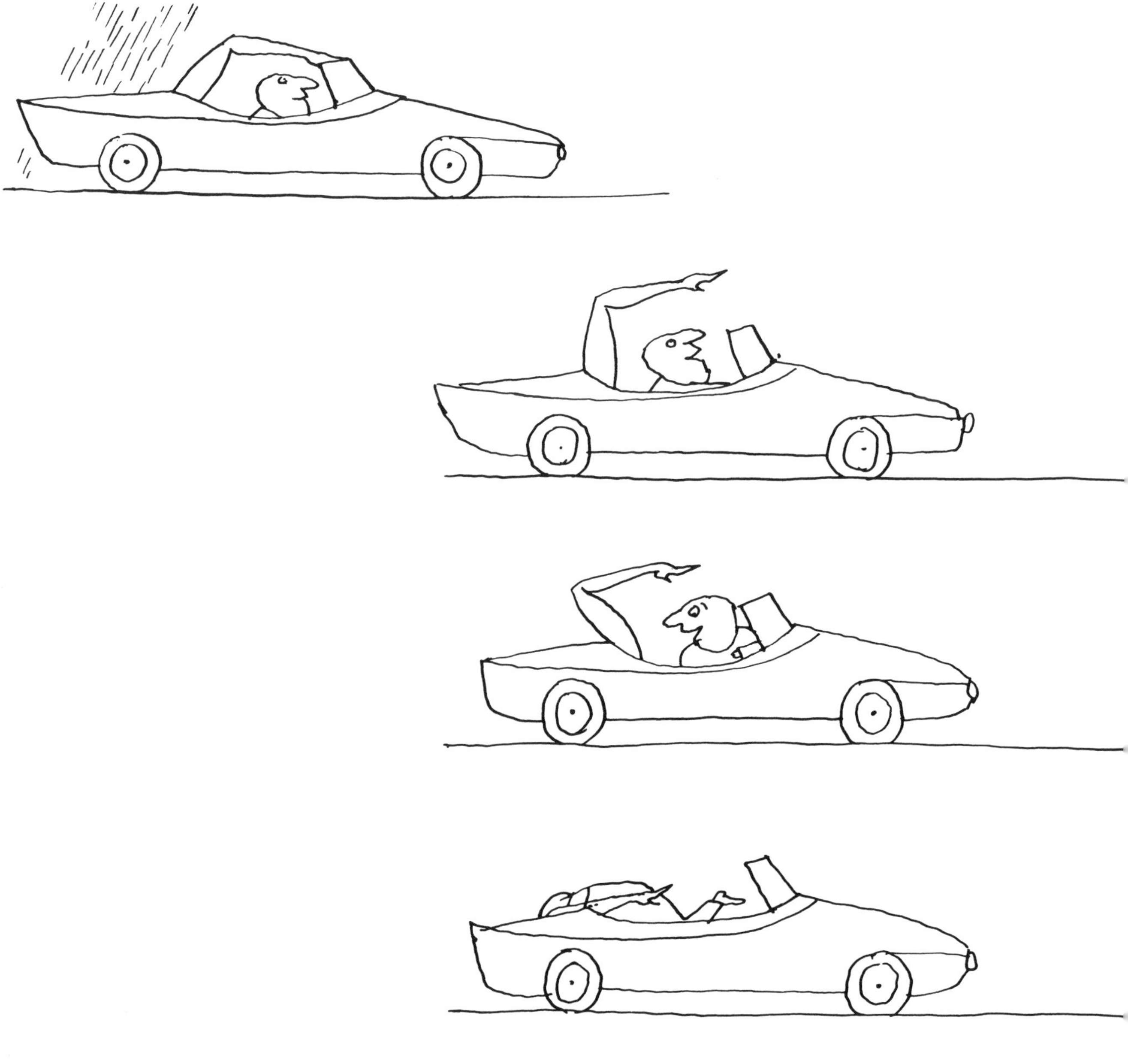

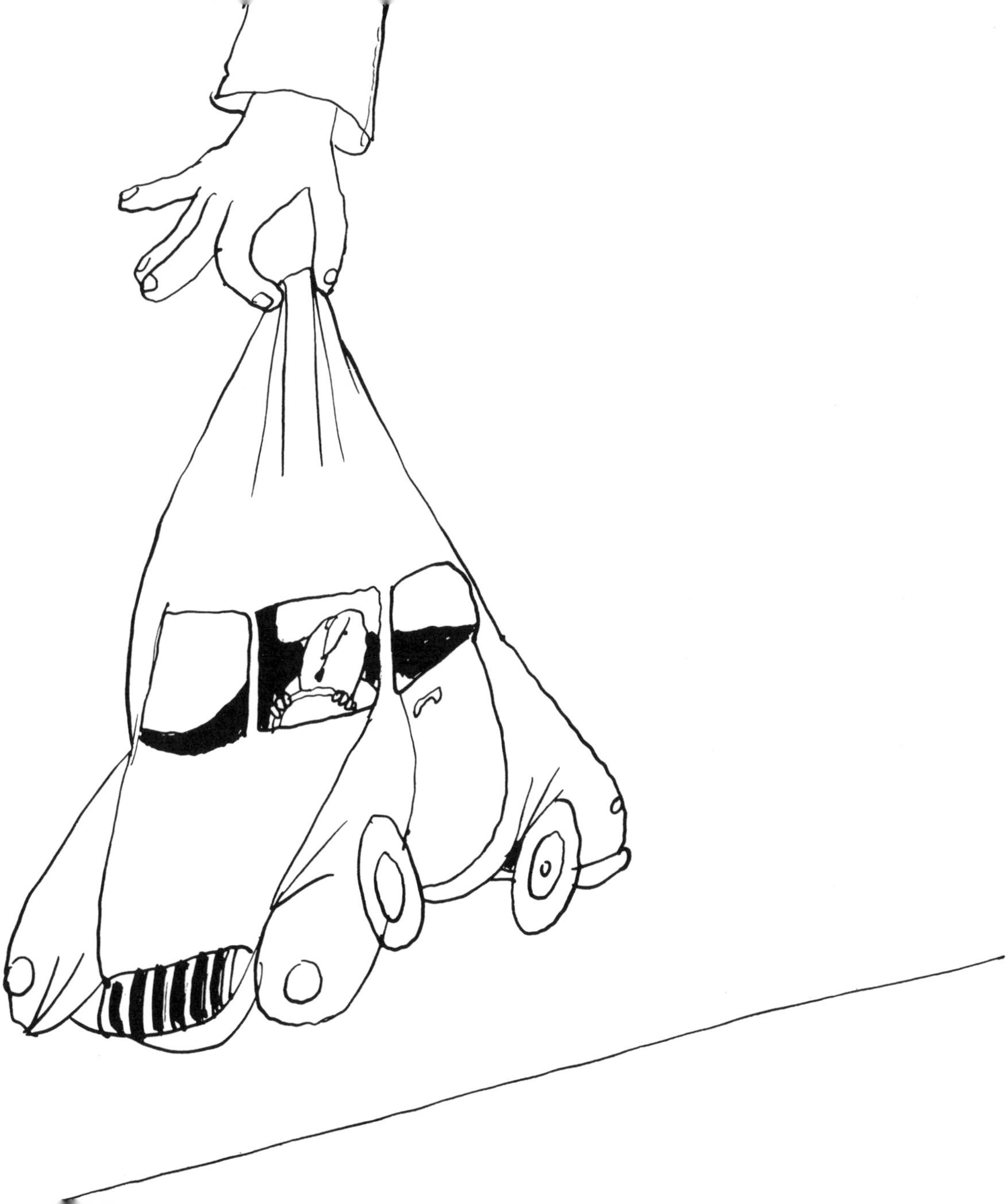

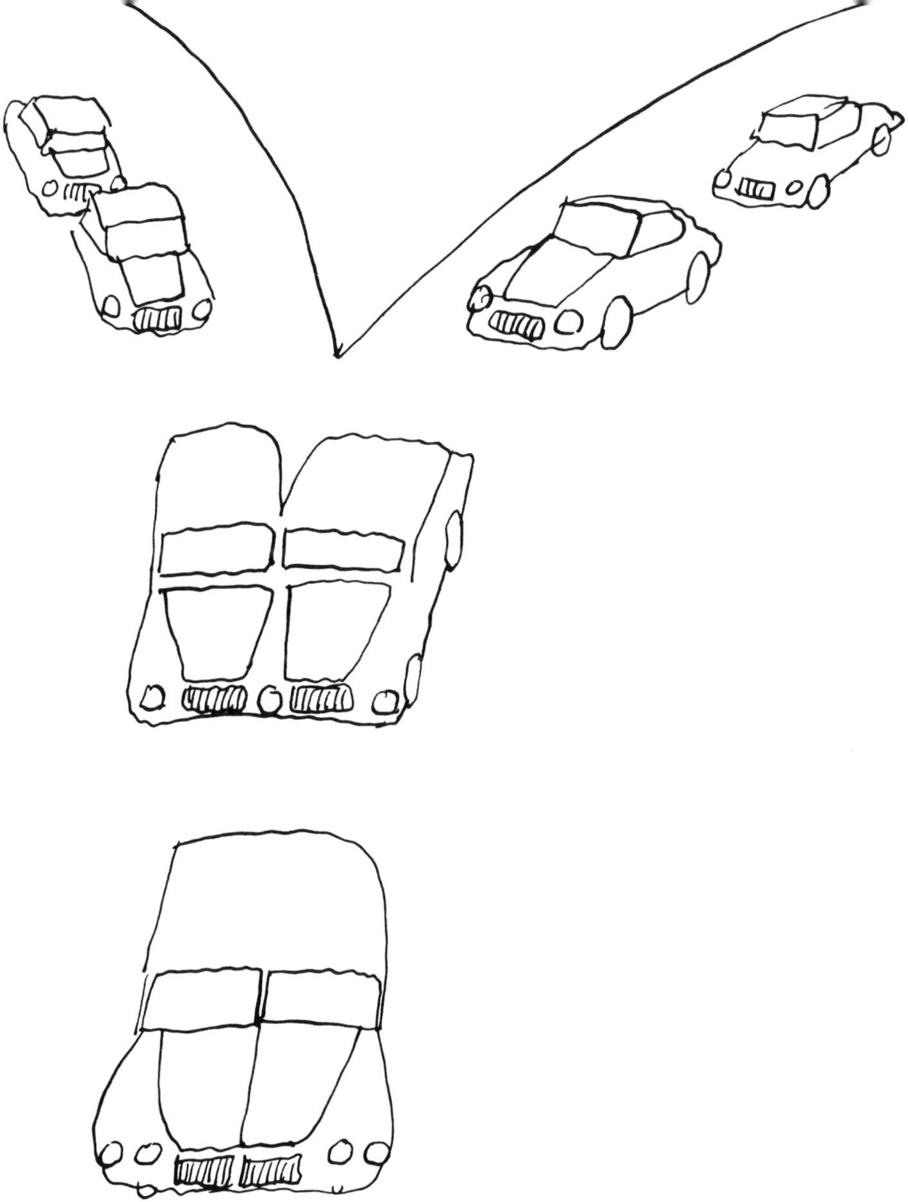

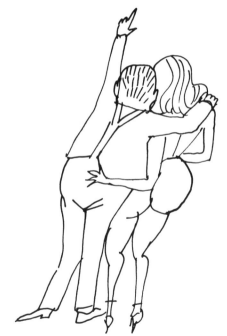

the exemple

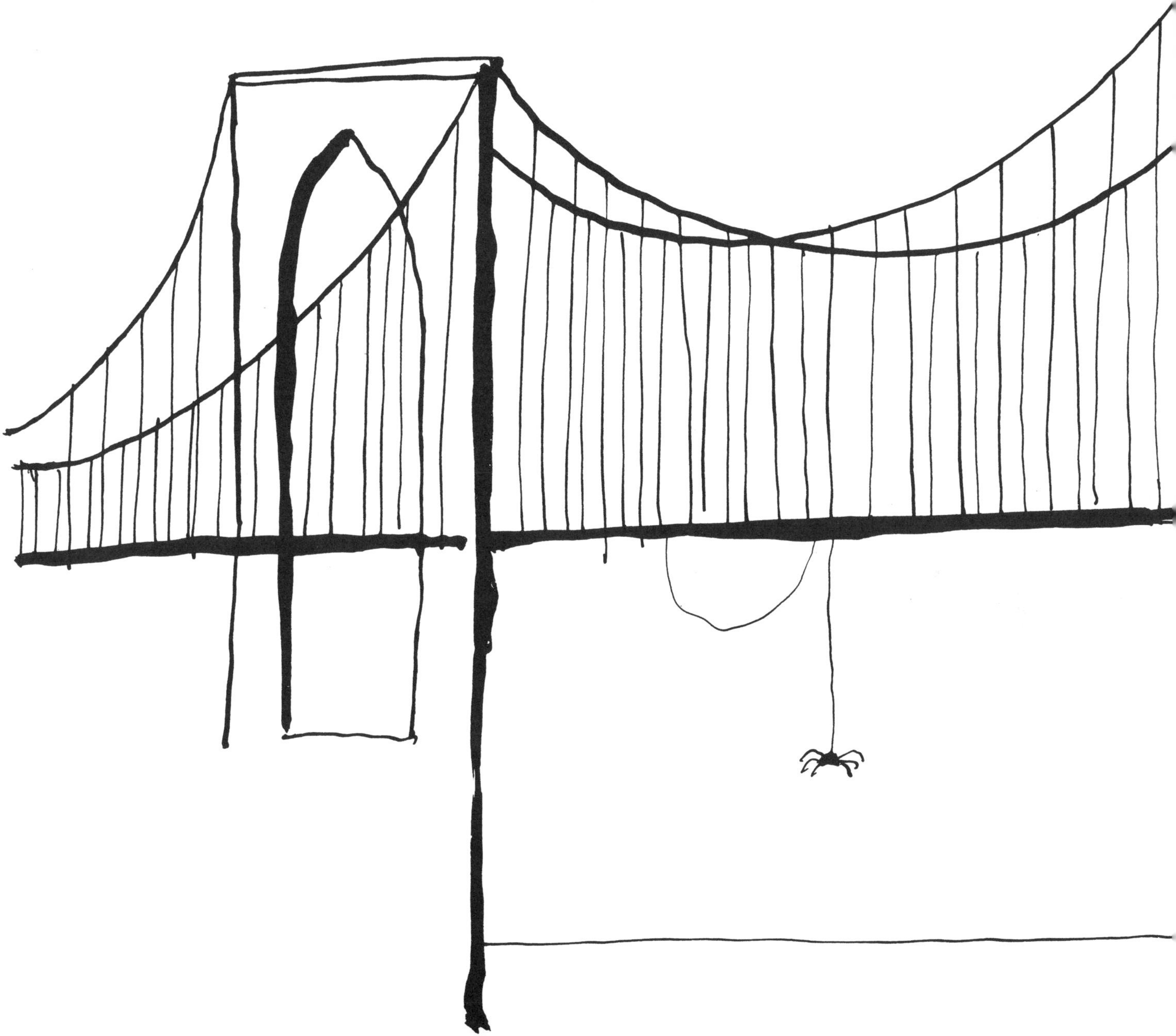

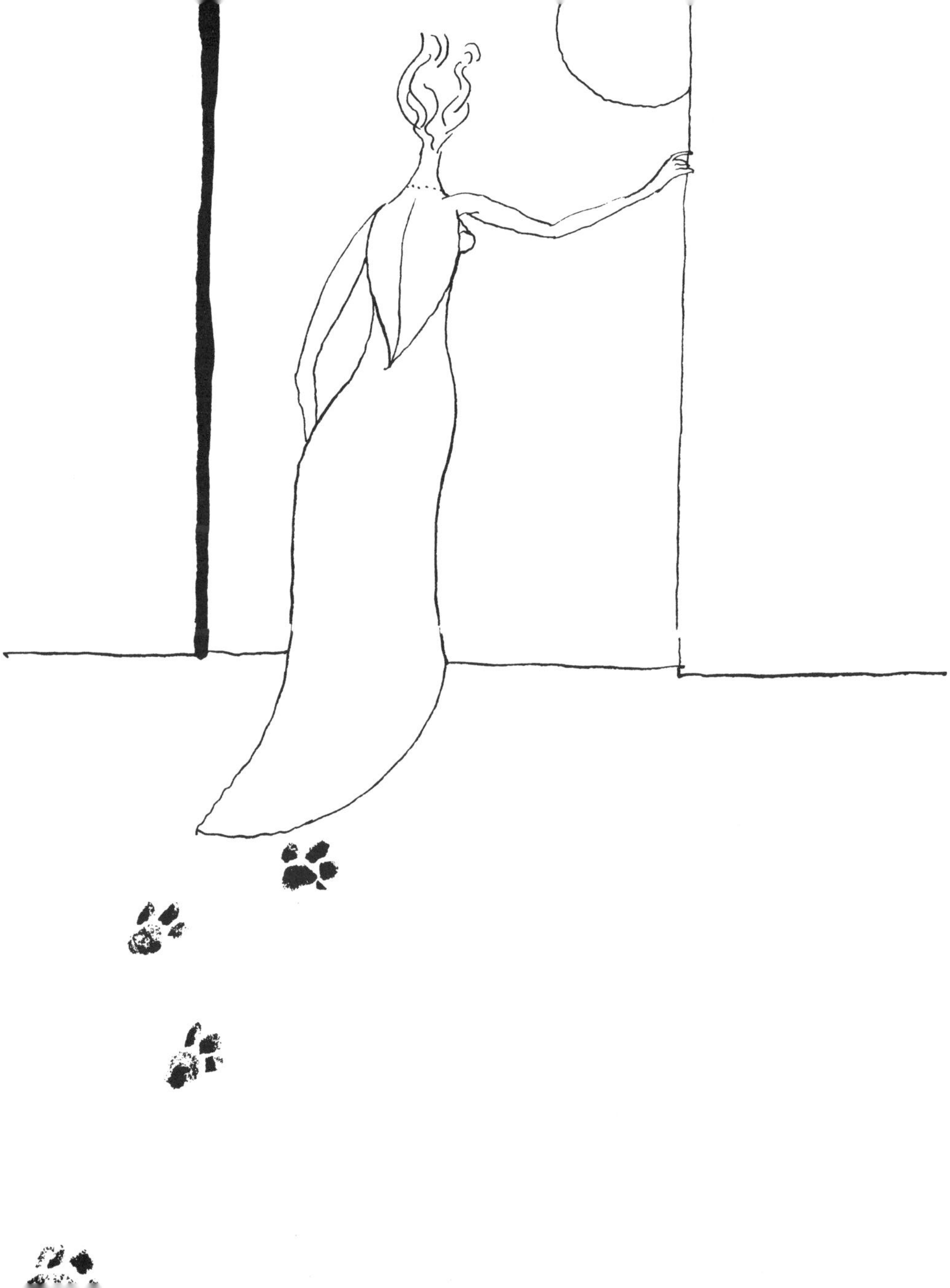

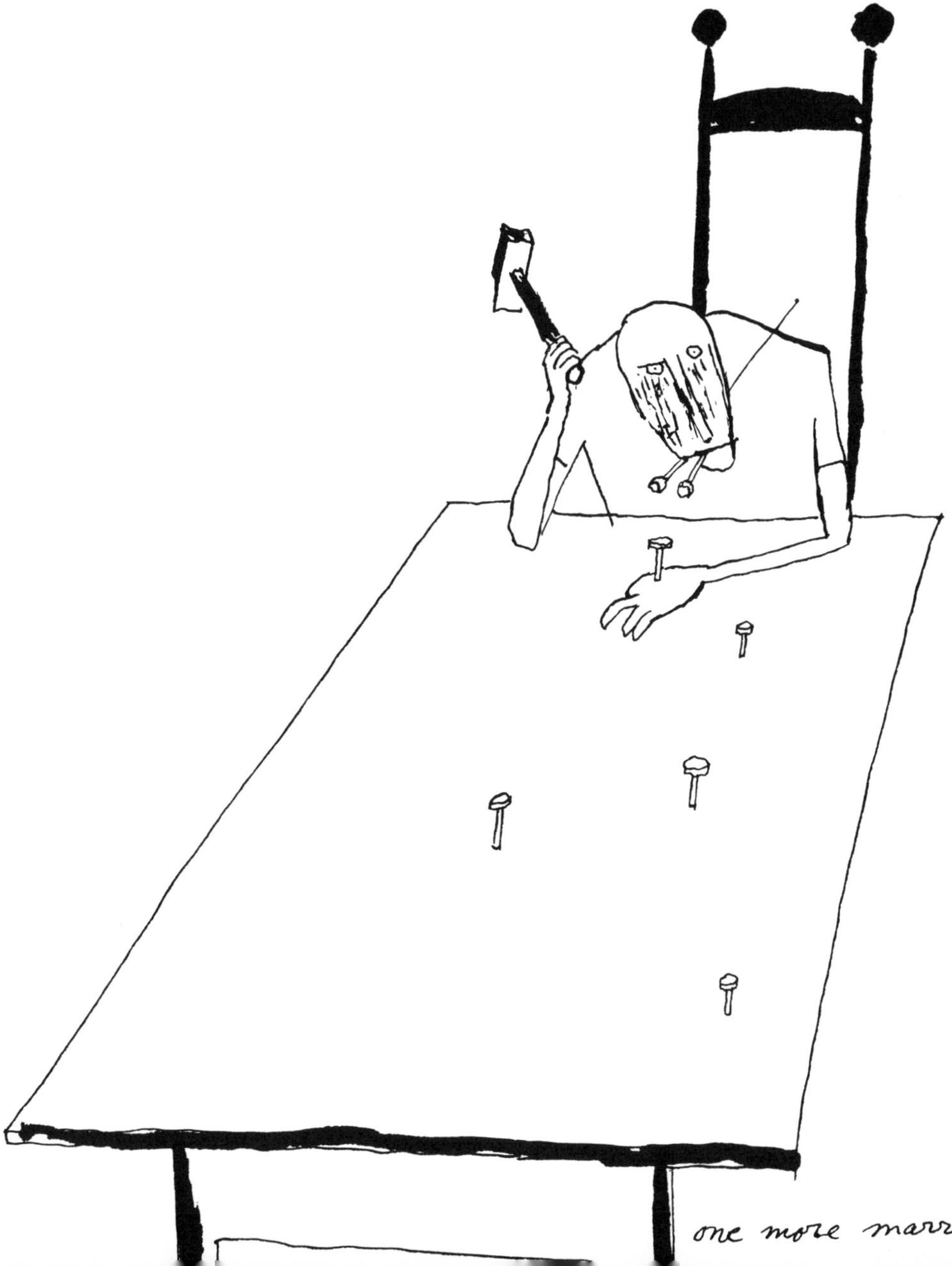

*one more marriage*

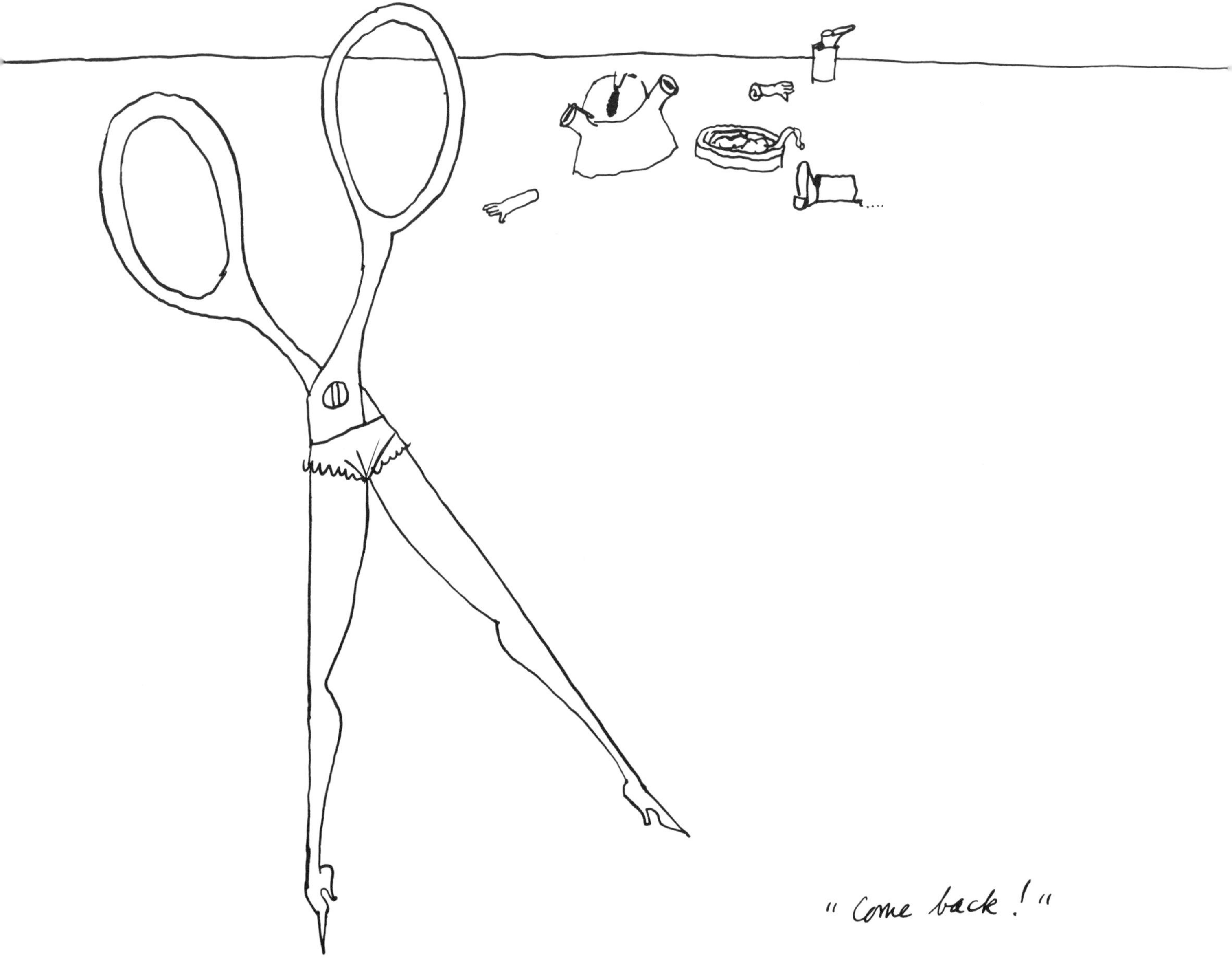

"Come back!"

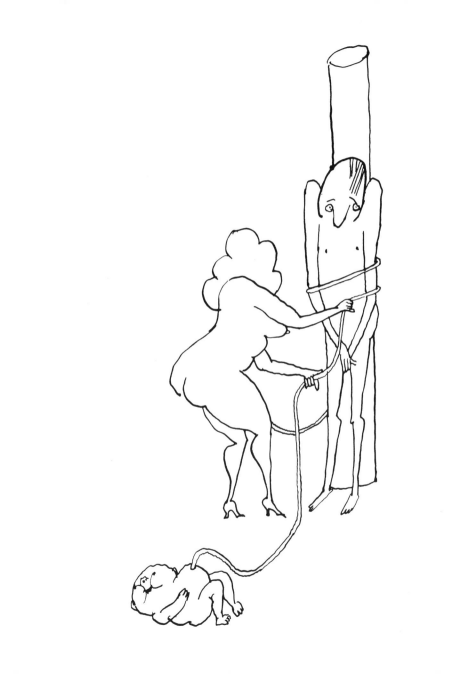

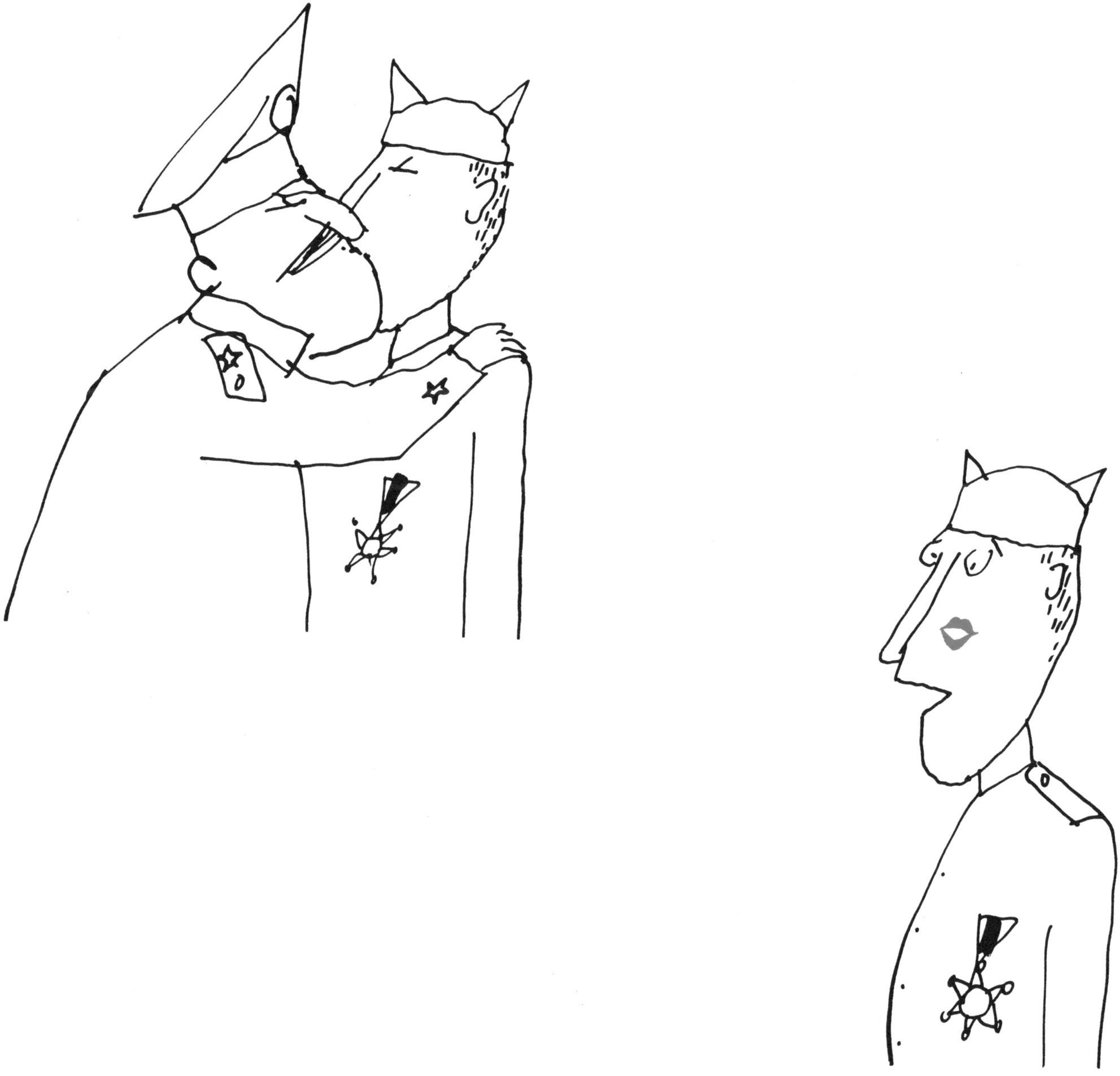

anti climax

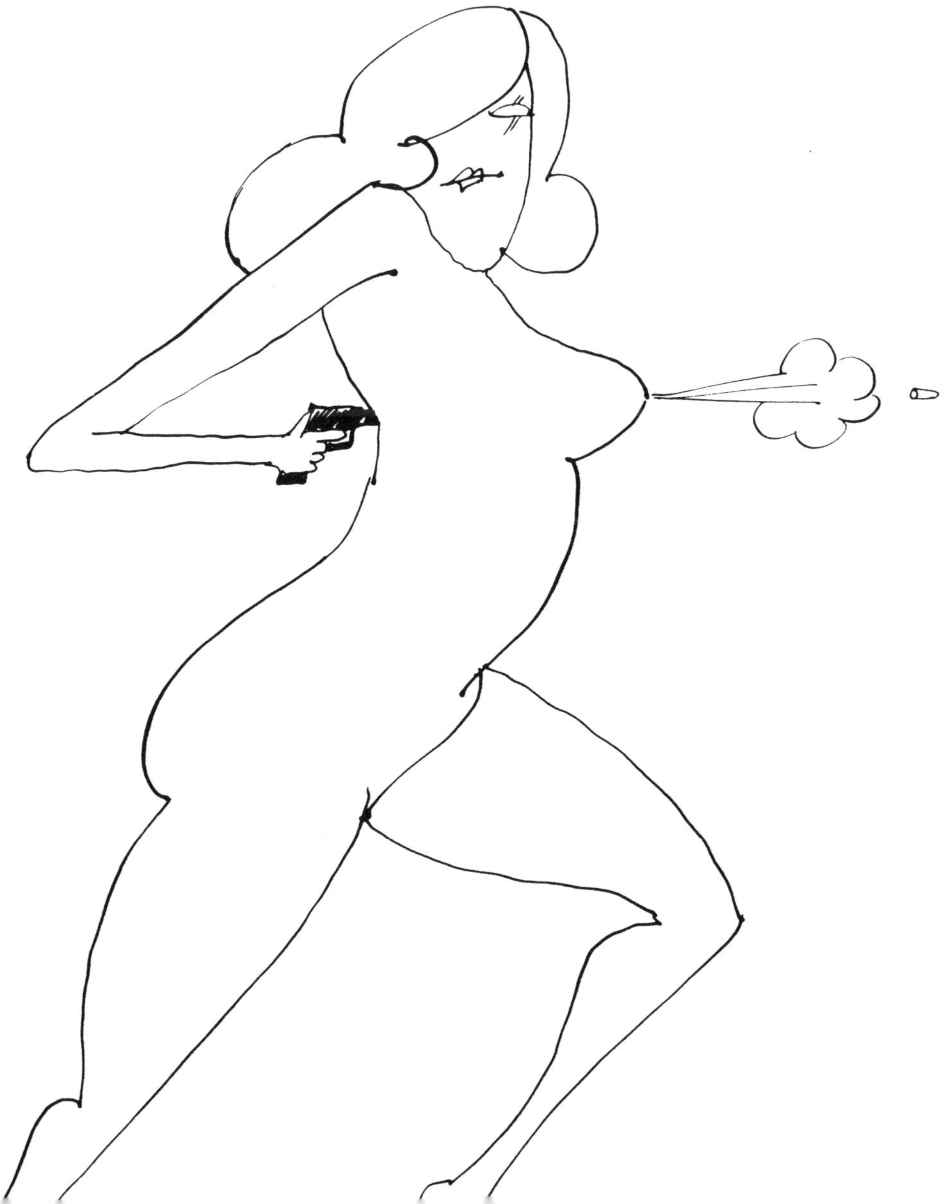

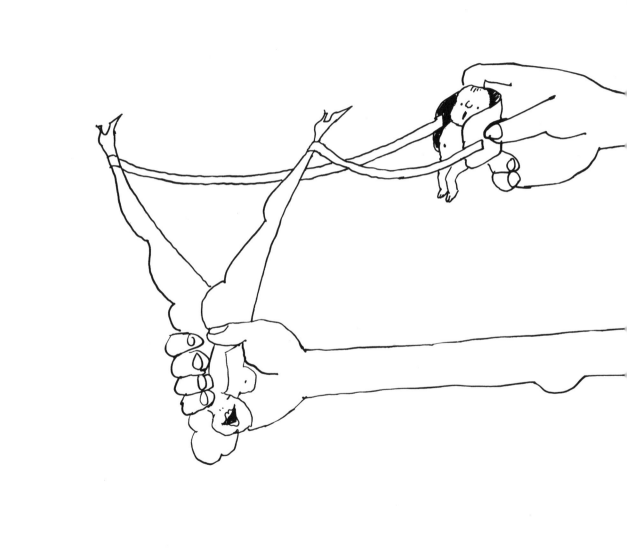

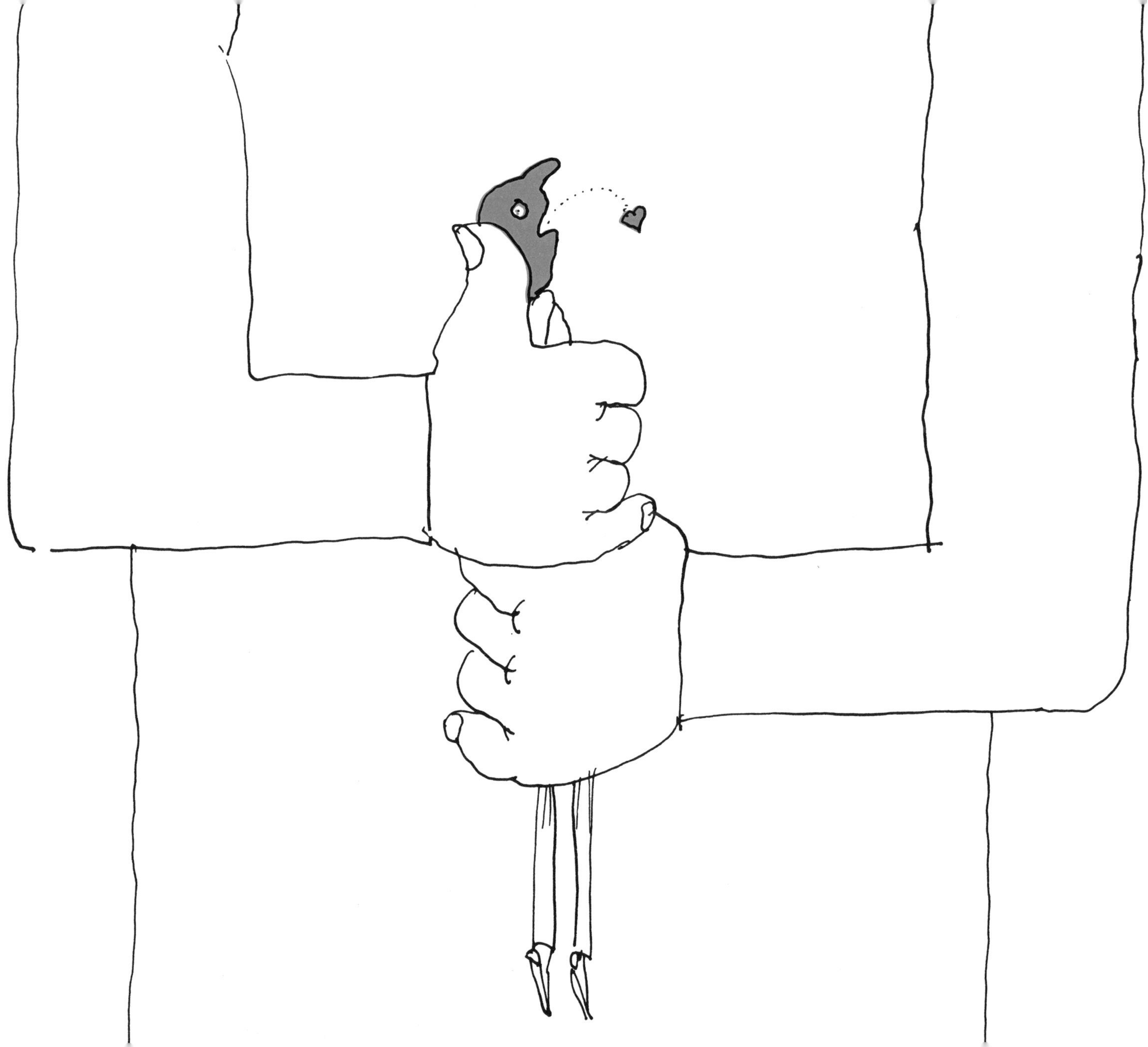

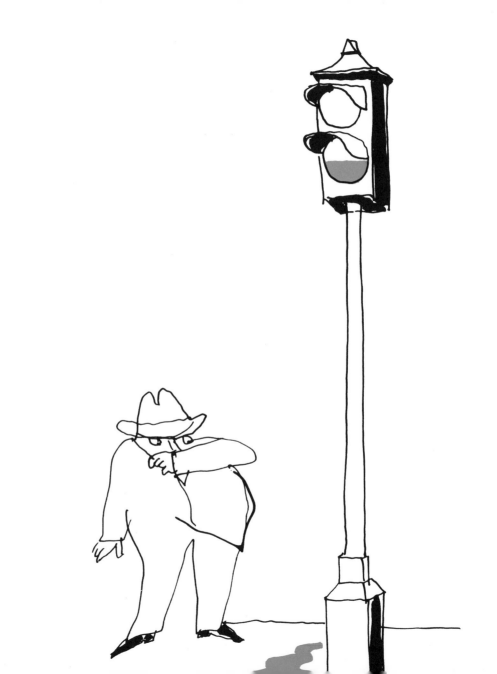

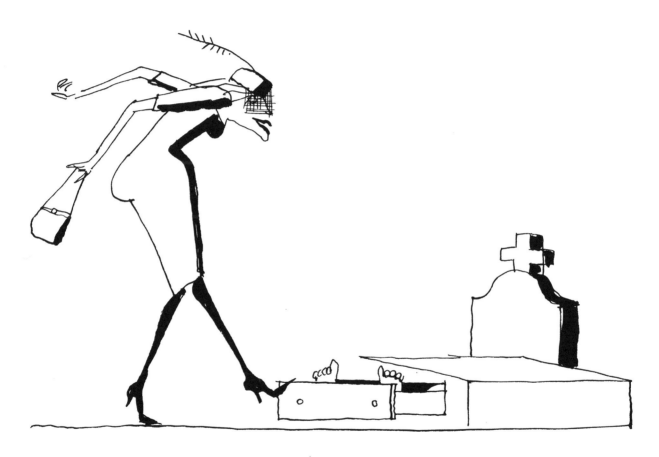

" Adieu ! "

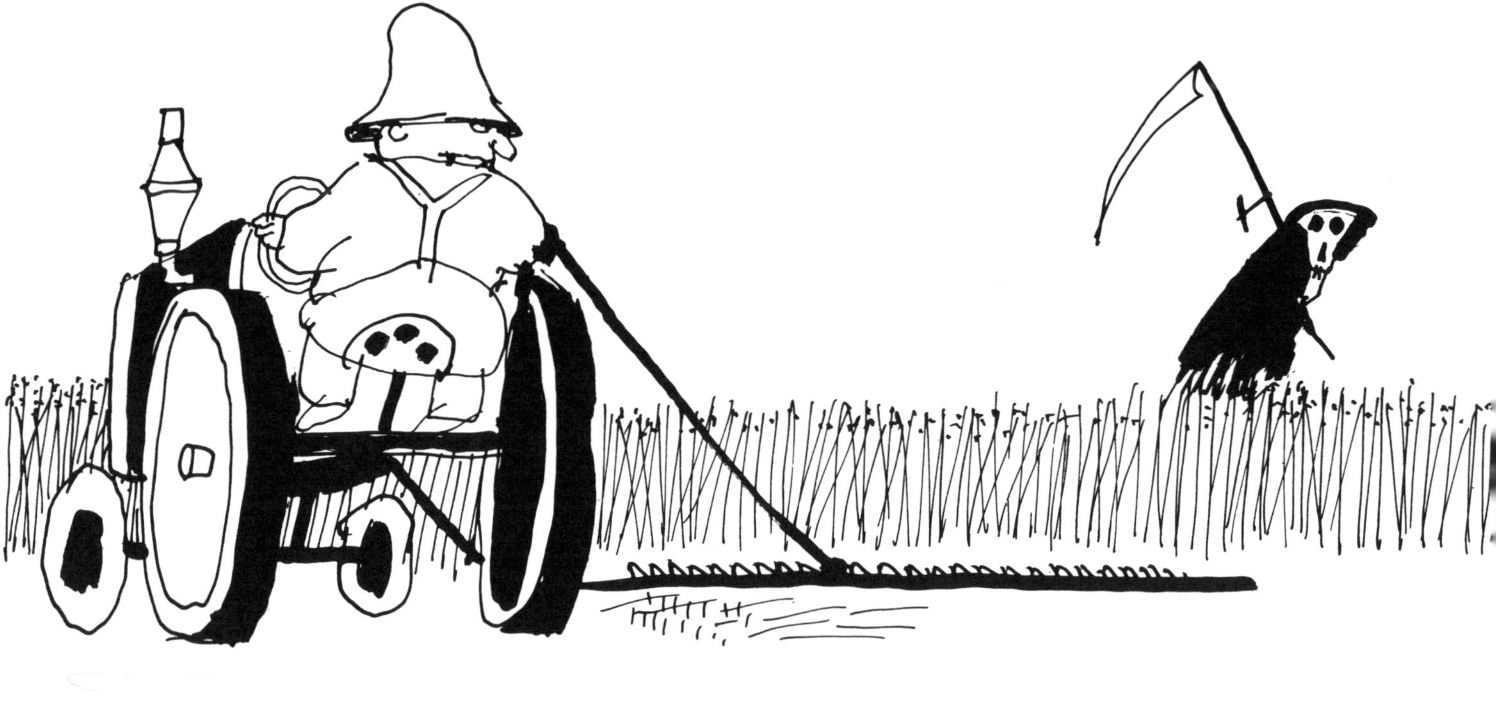

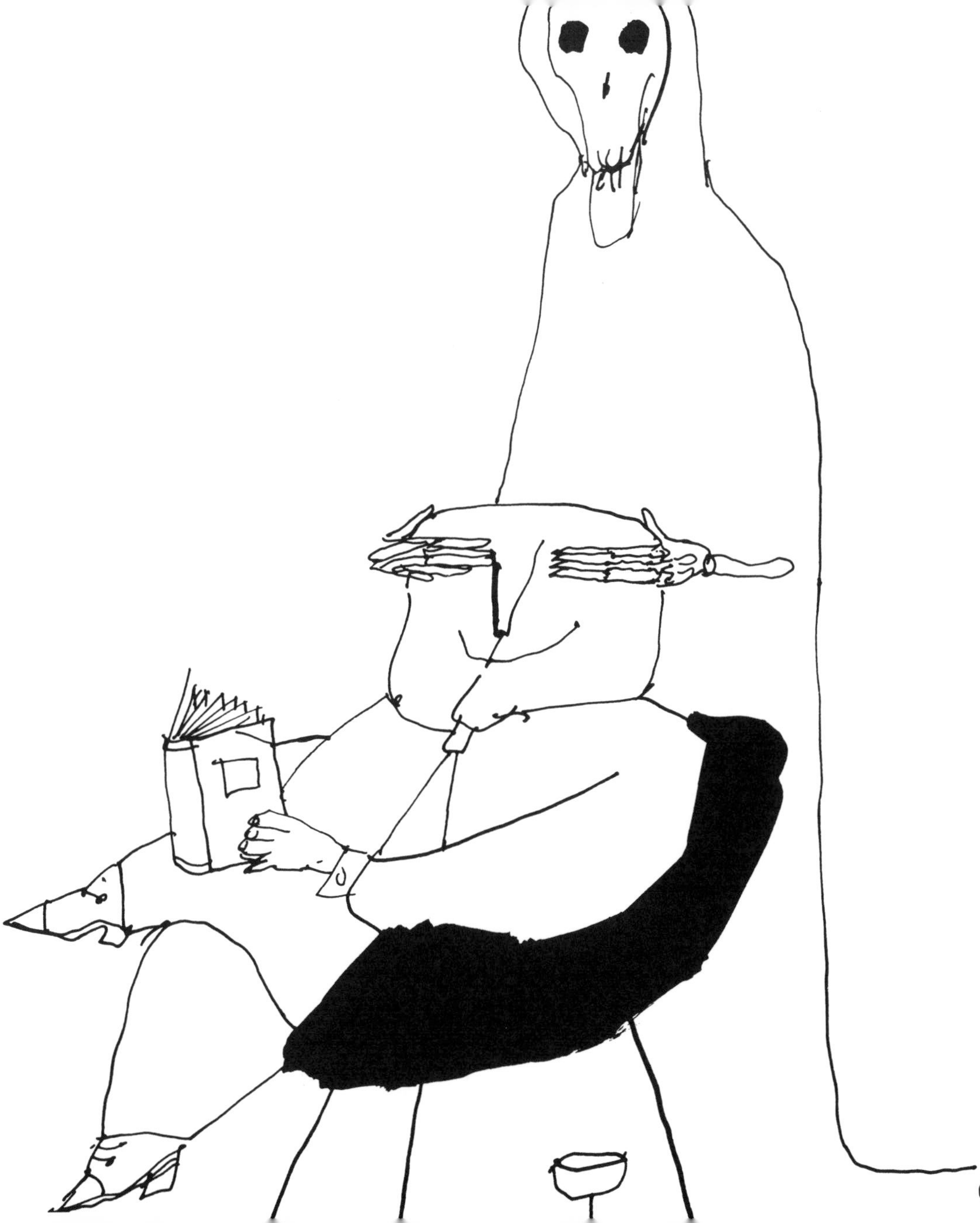

guess who ?

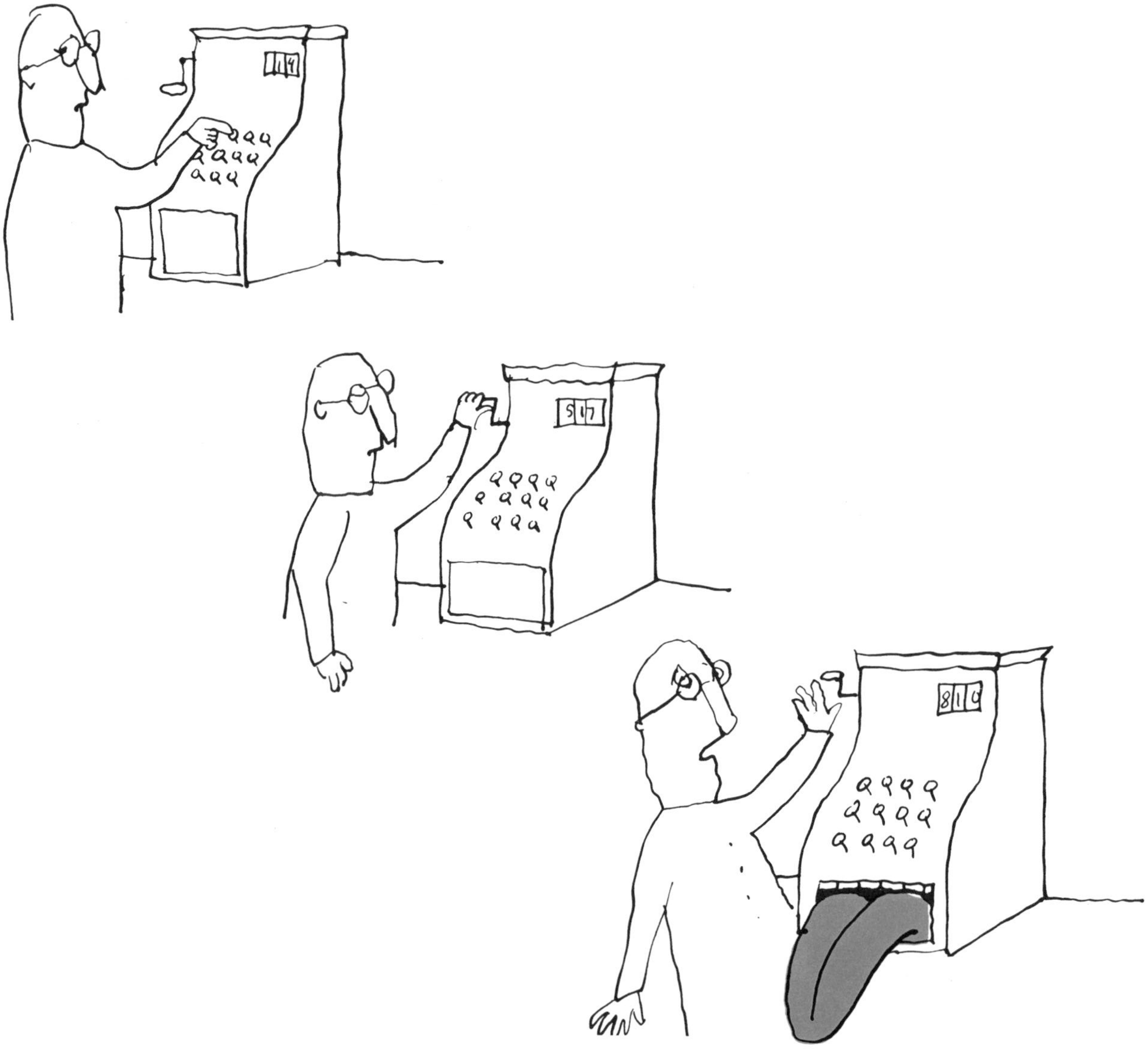

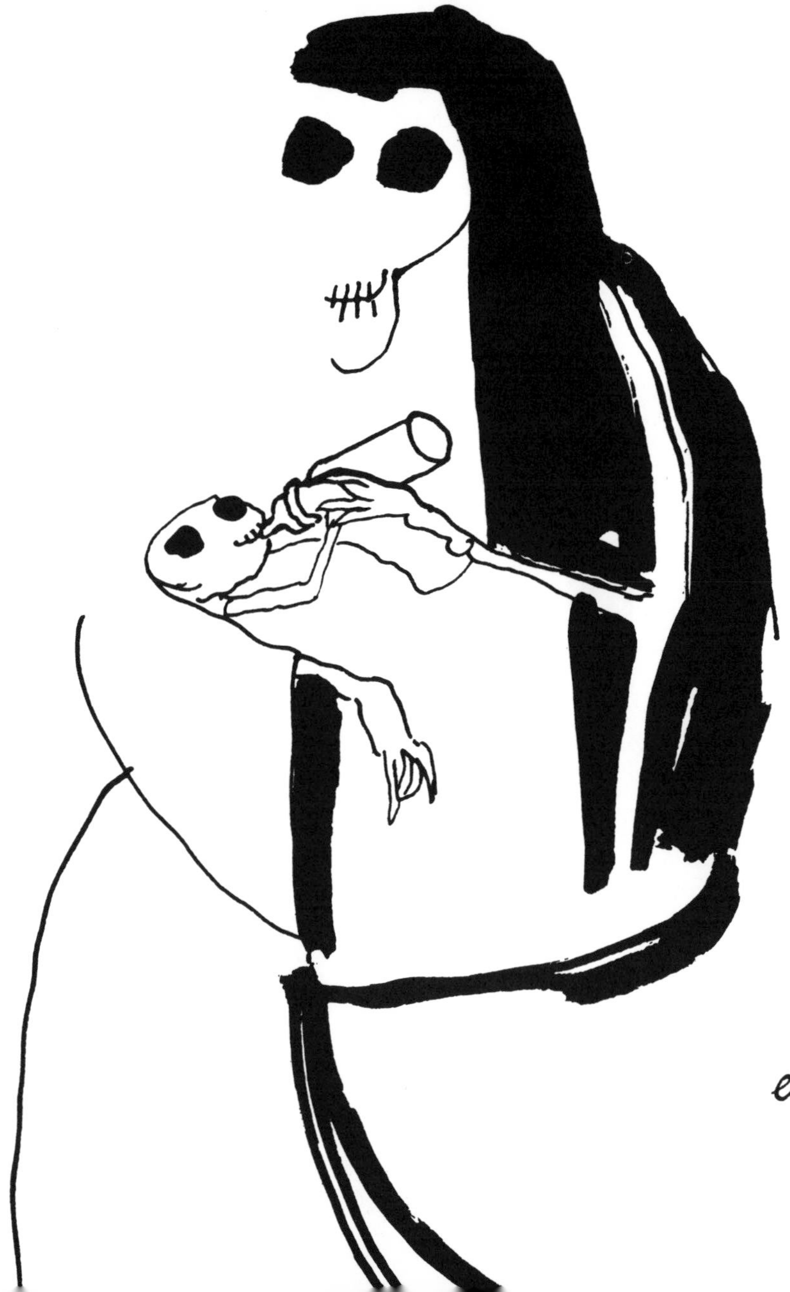

enfant du siècle

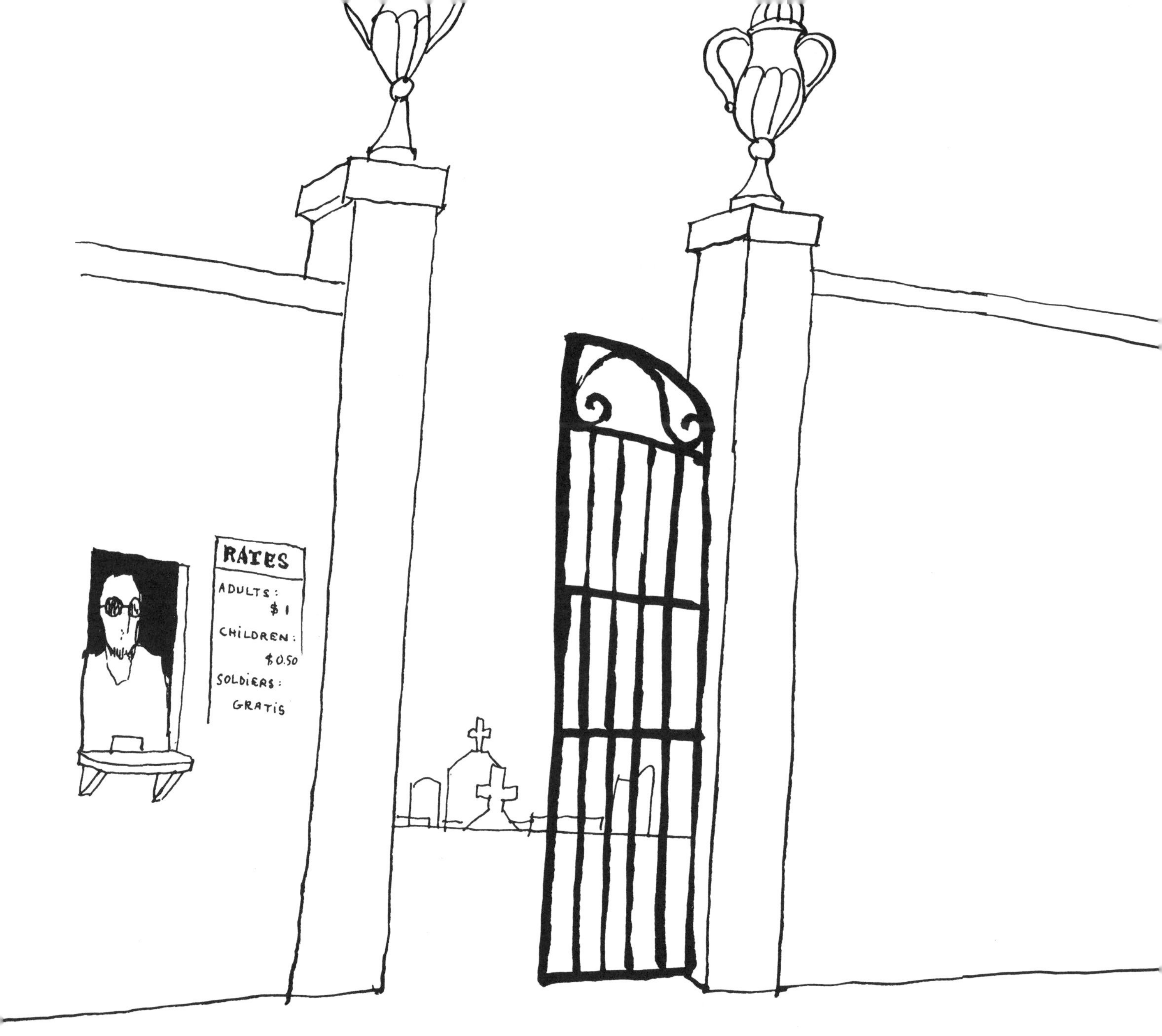
RATES
ADULTS: $1
CHILDREN: $0.50
SOLDIERS: GRATIS

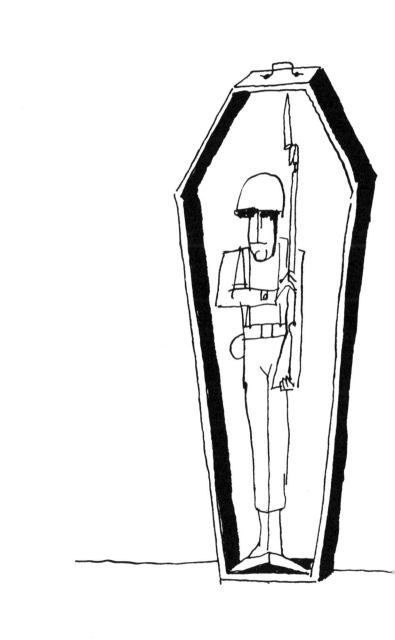

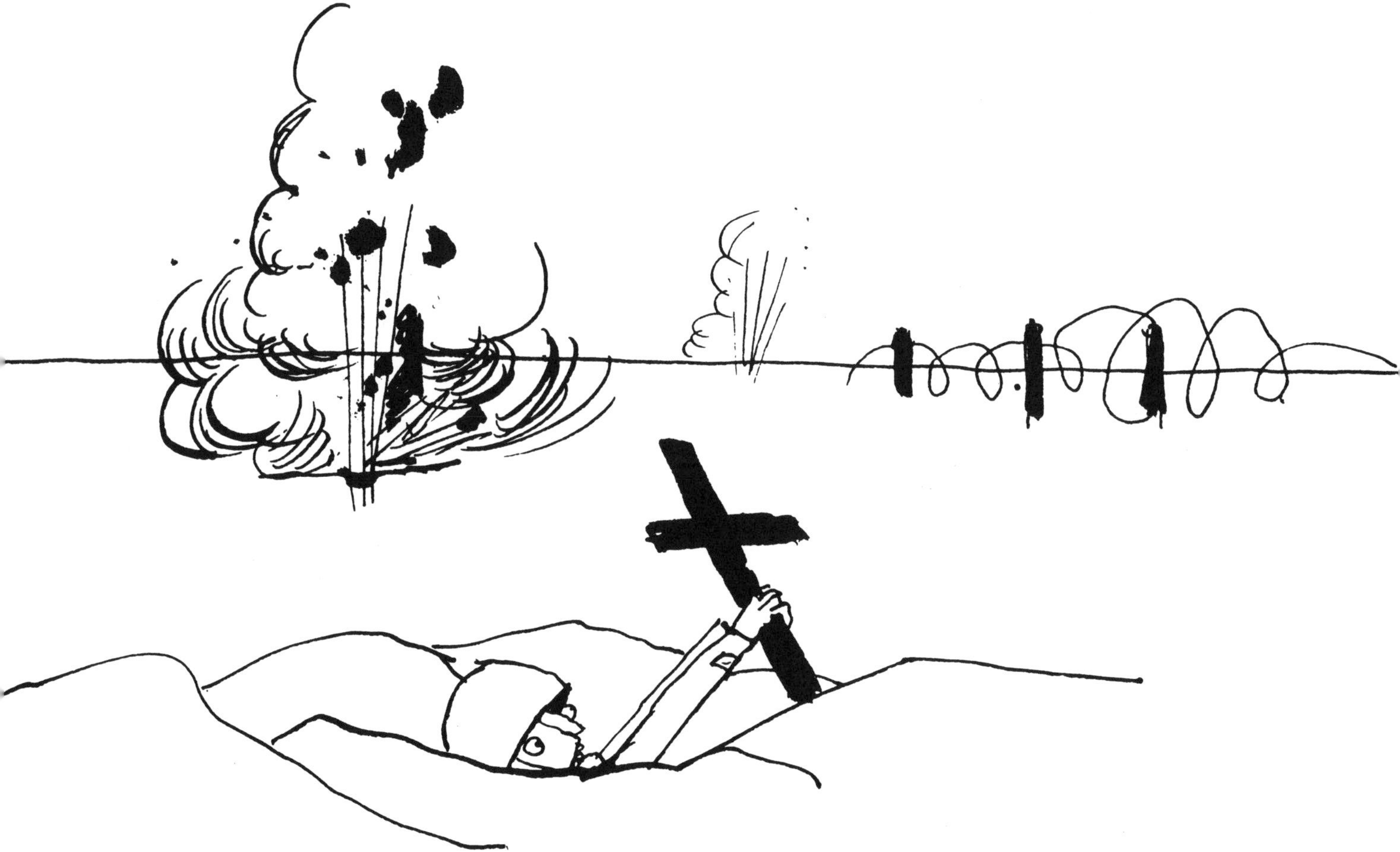

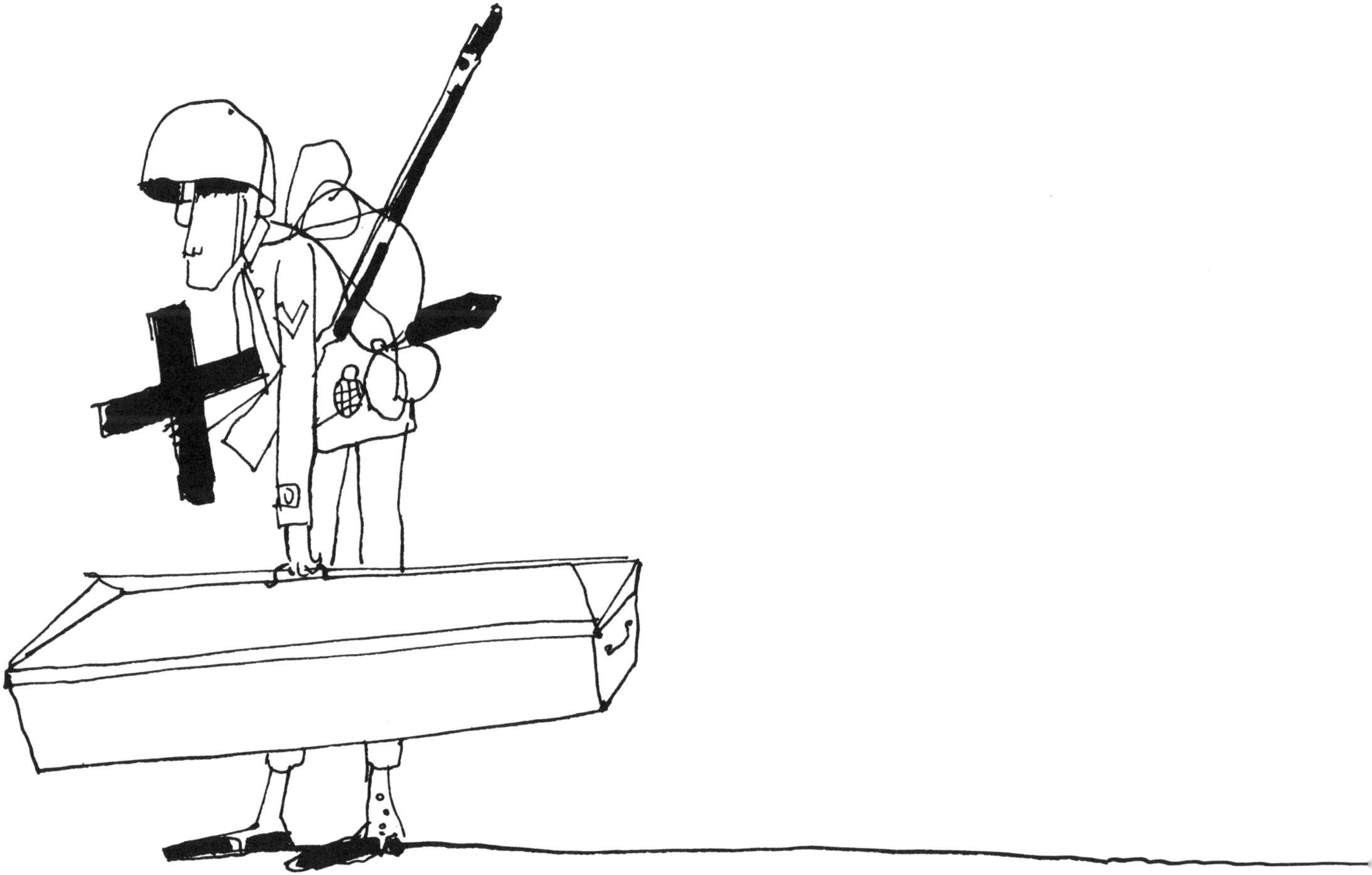

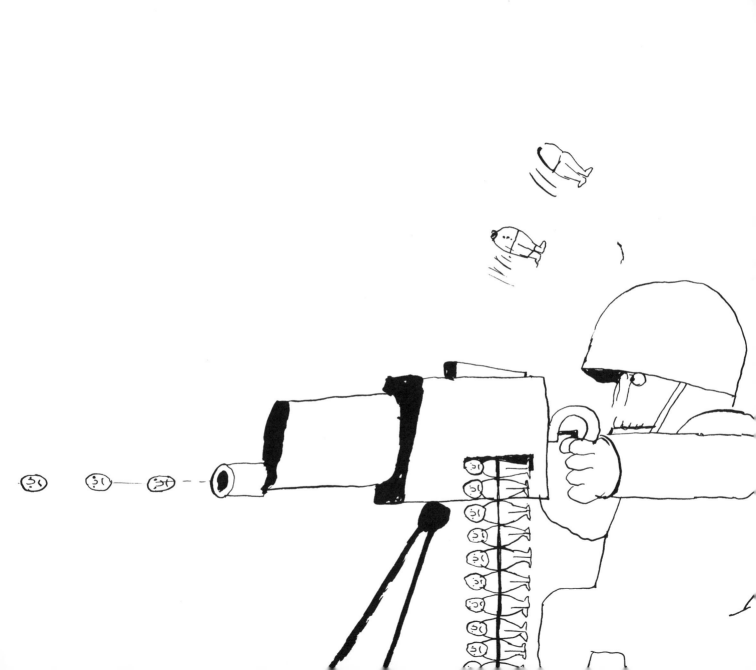

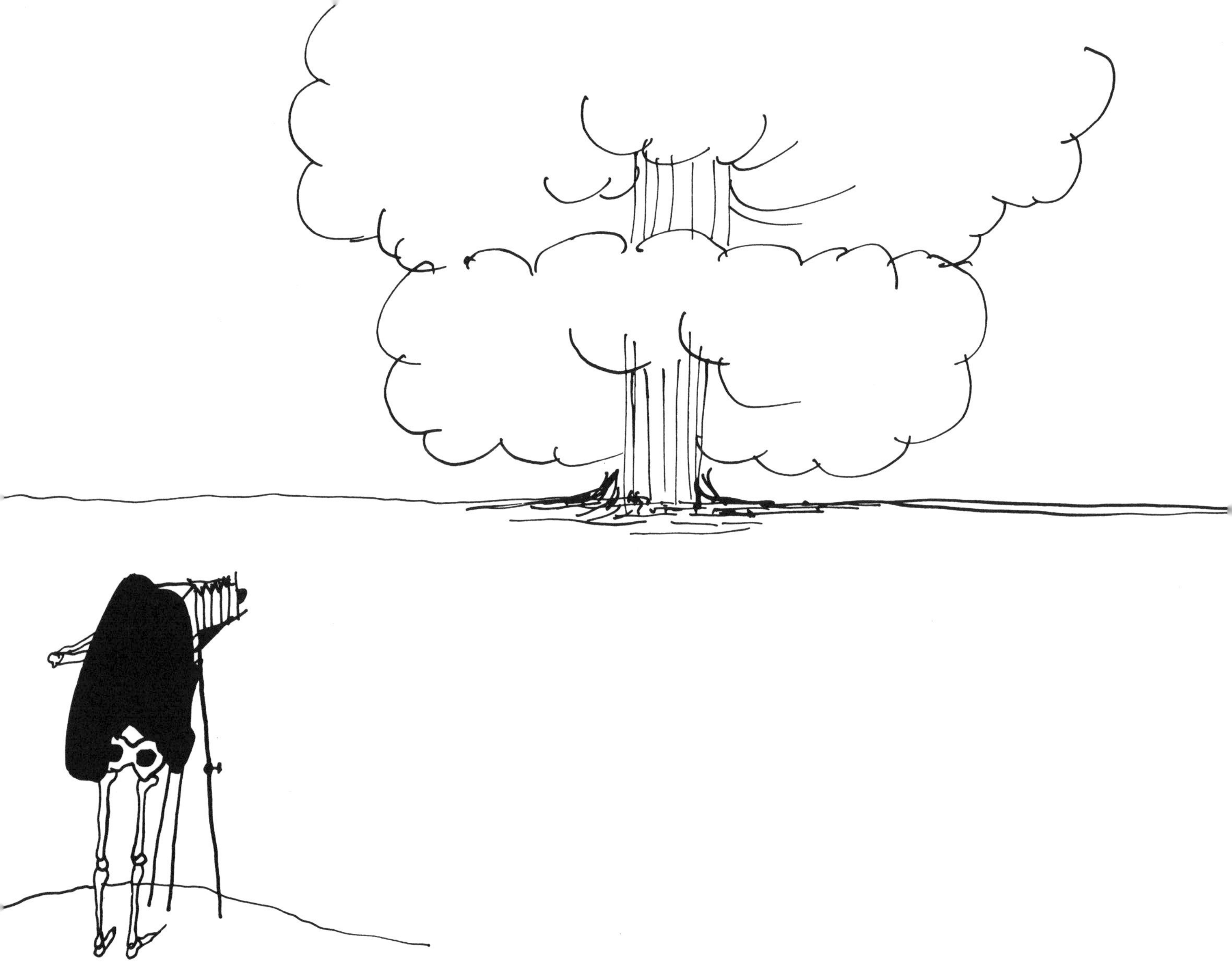

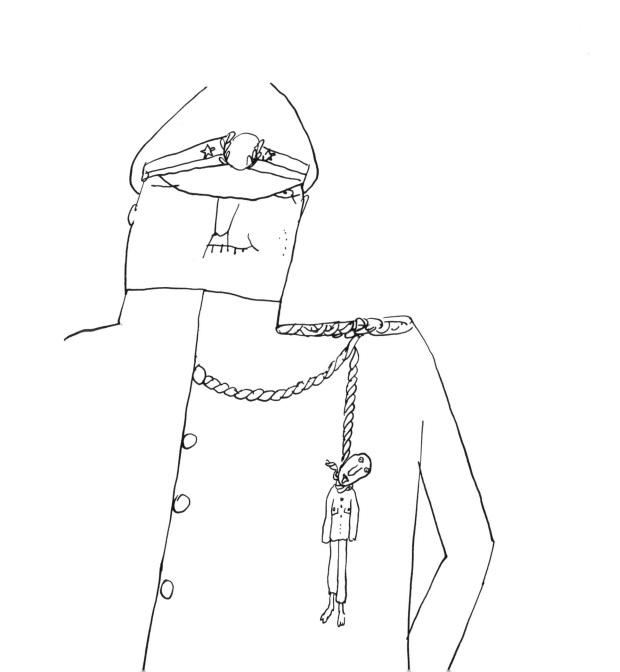

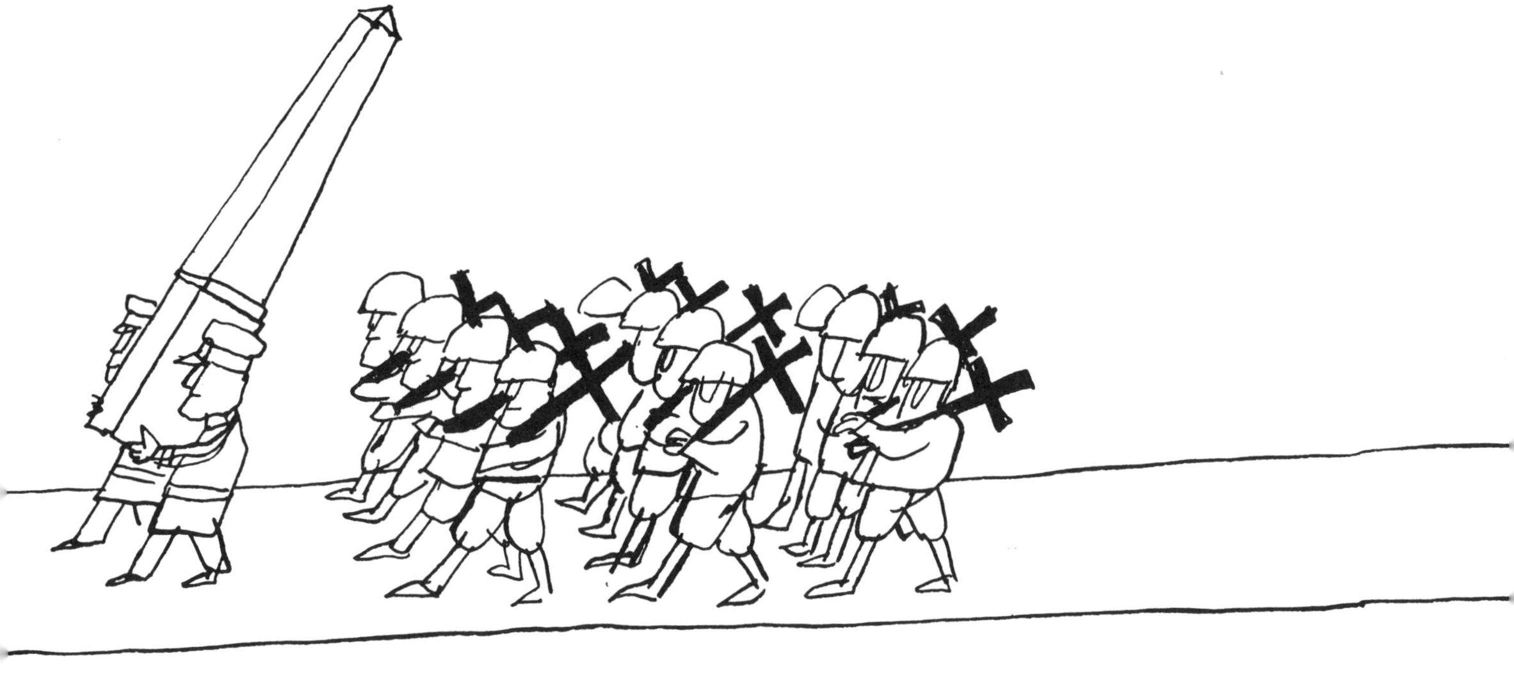

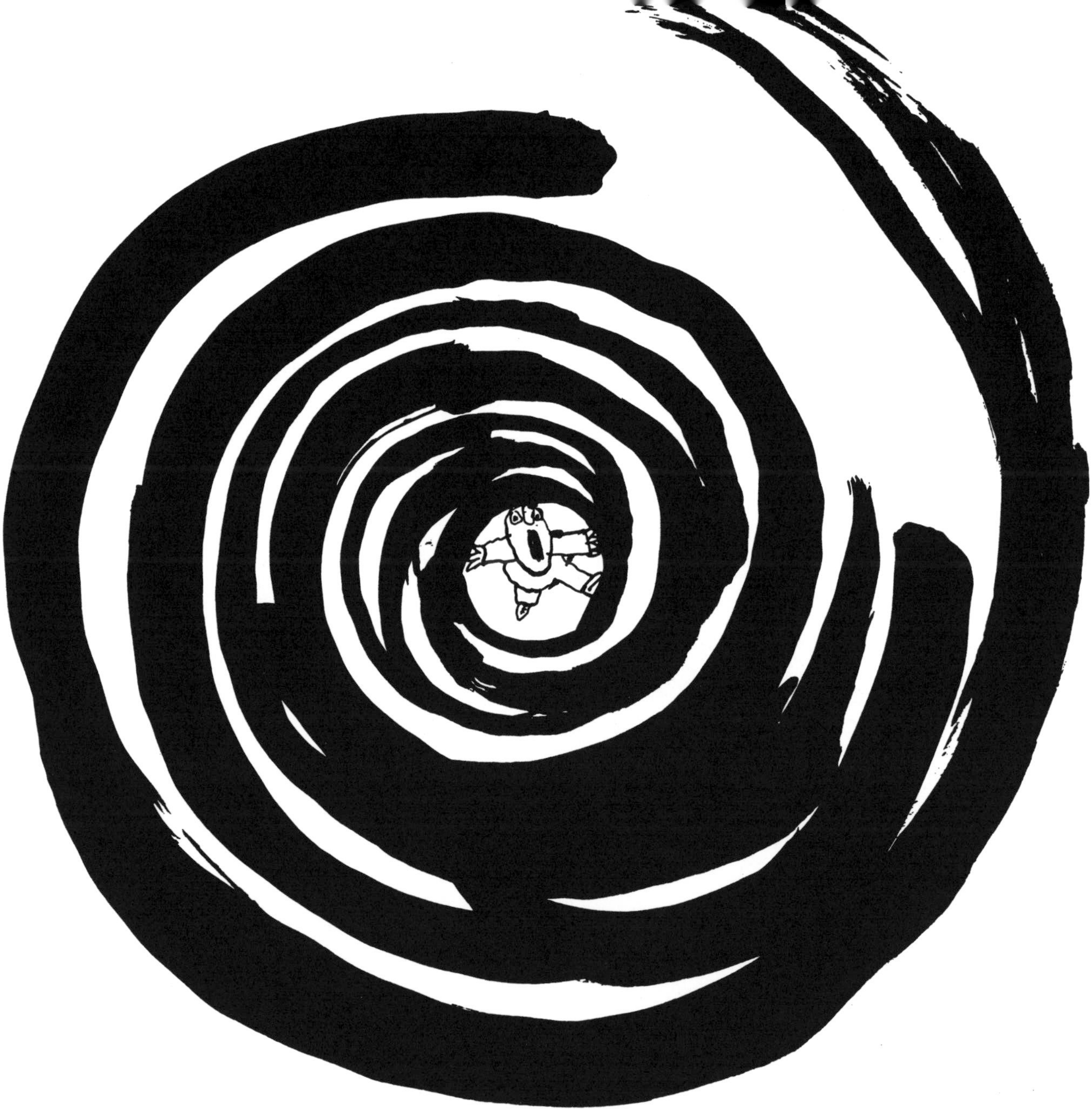

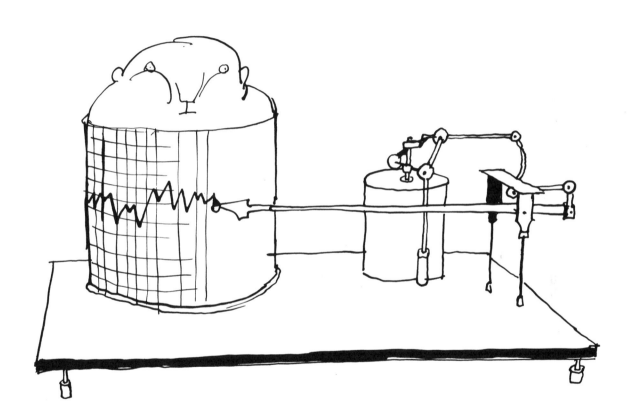

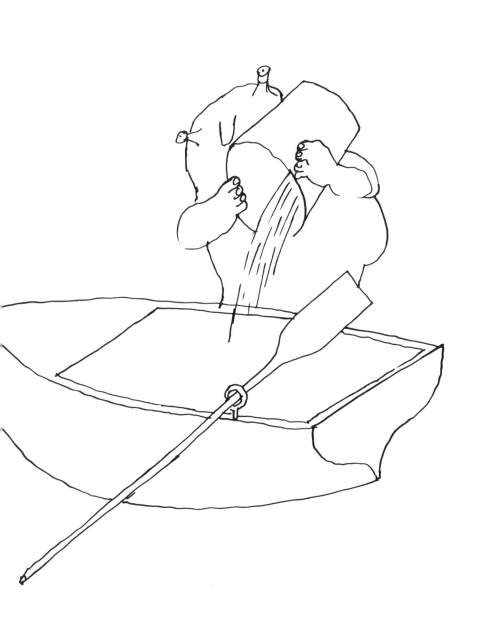

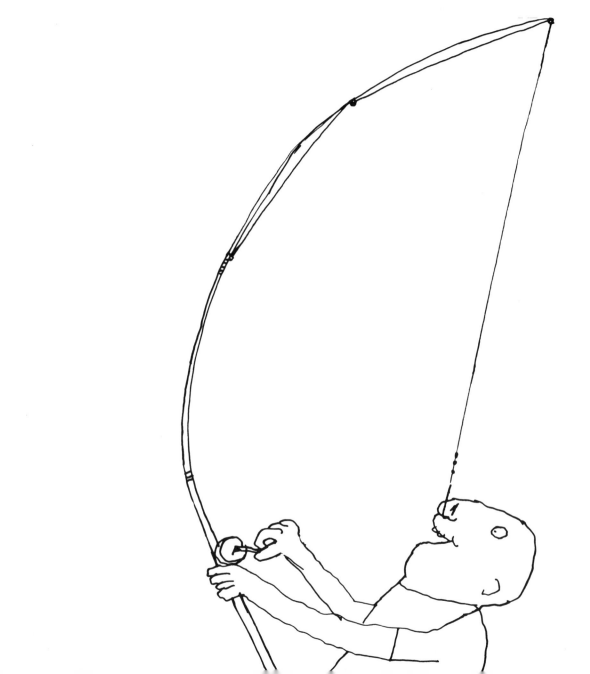

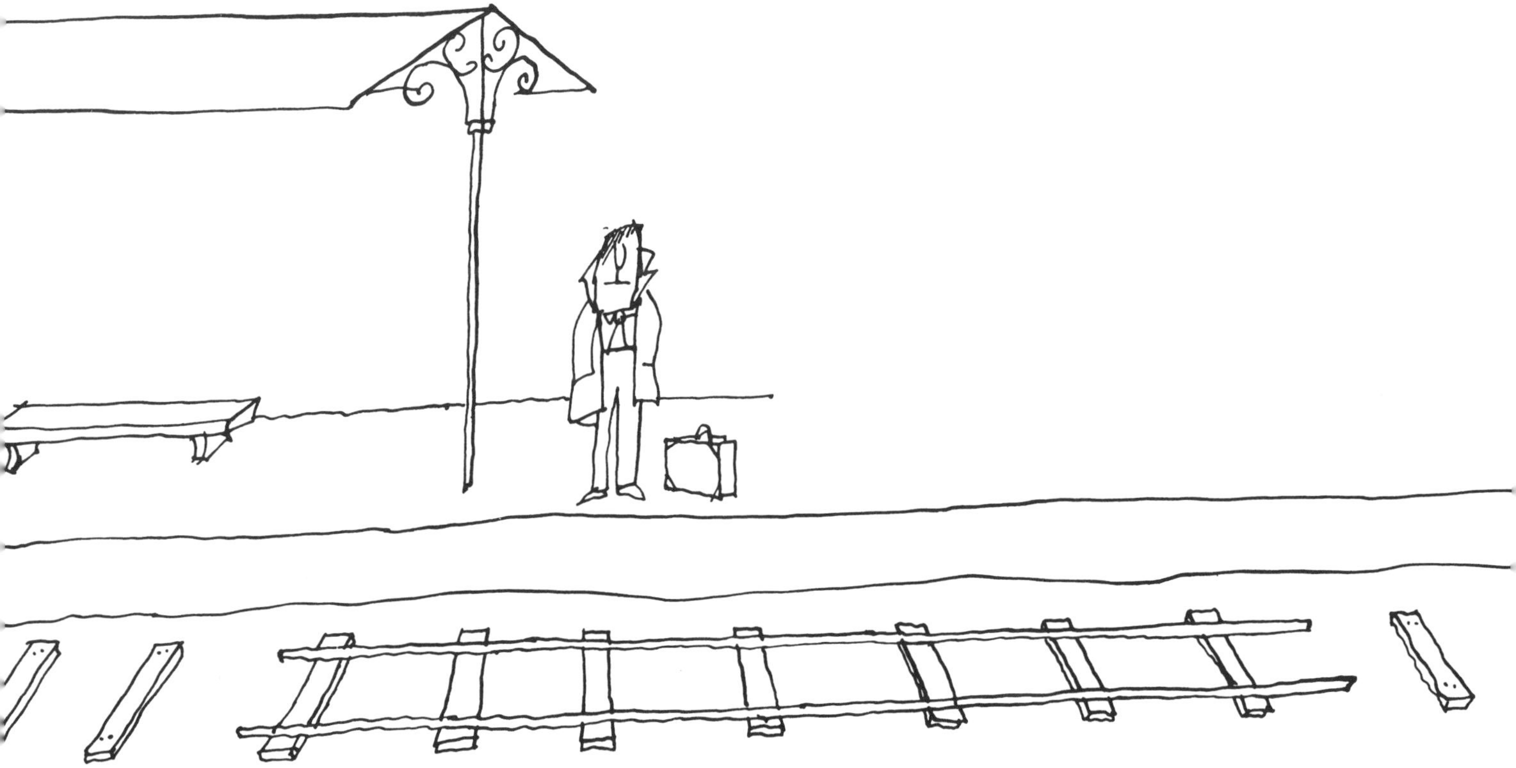

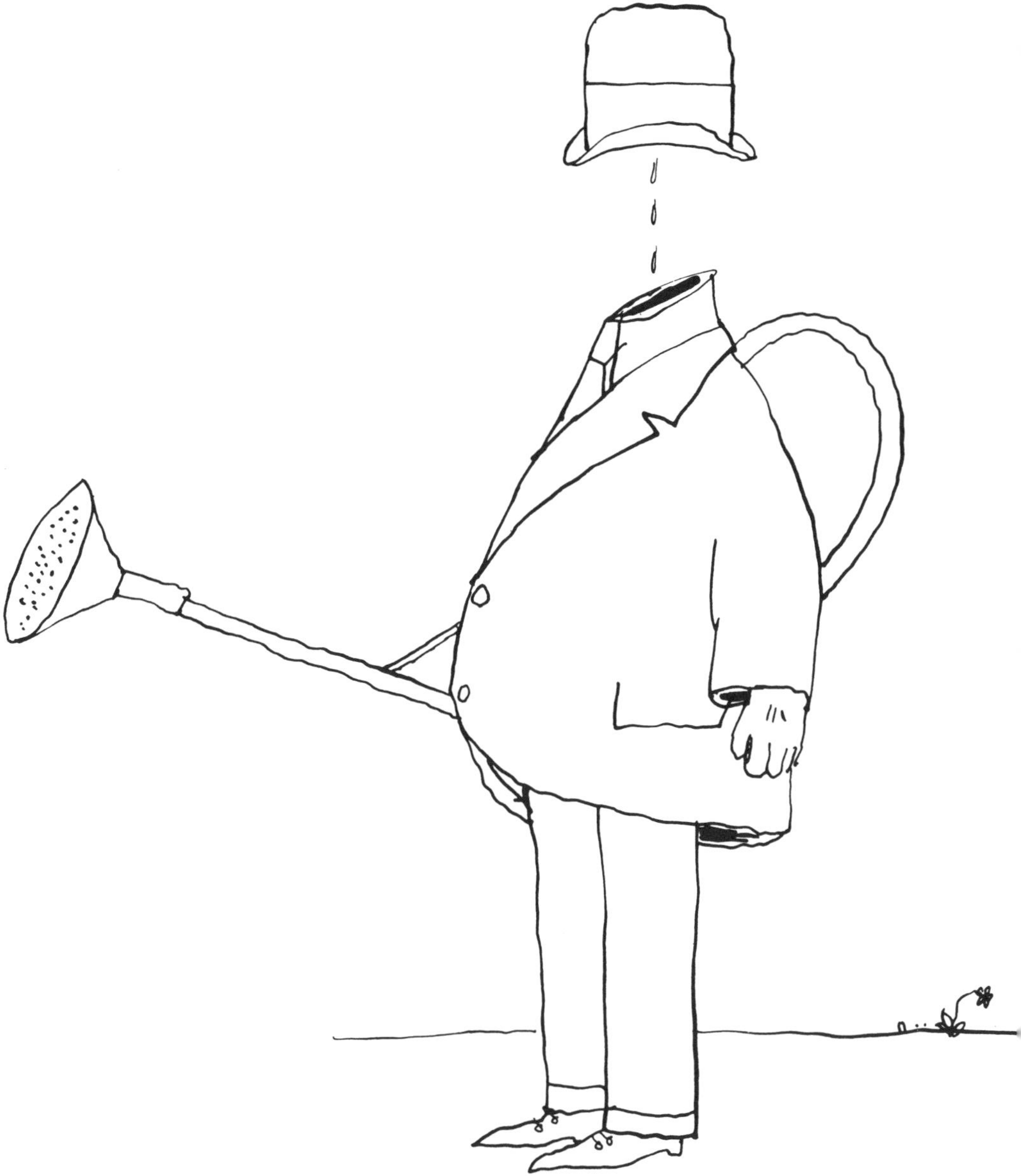

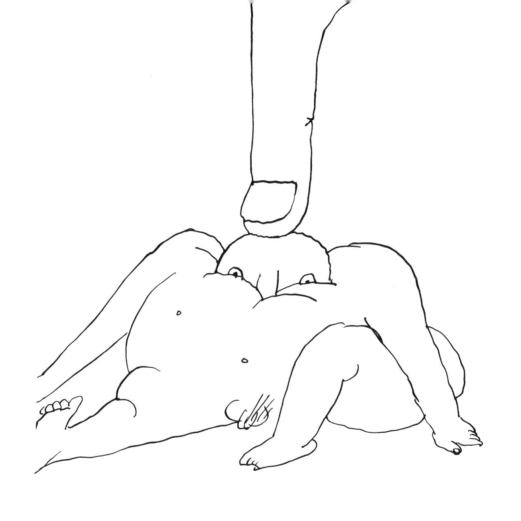

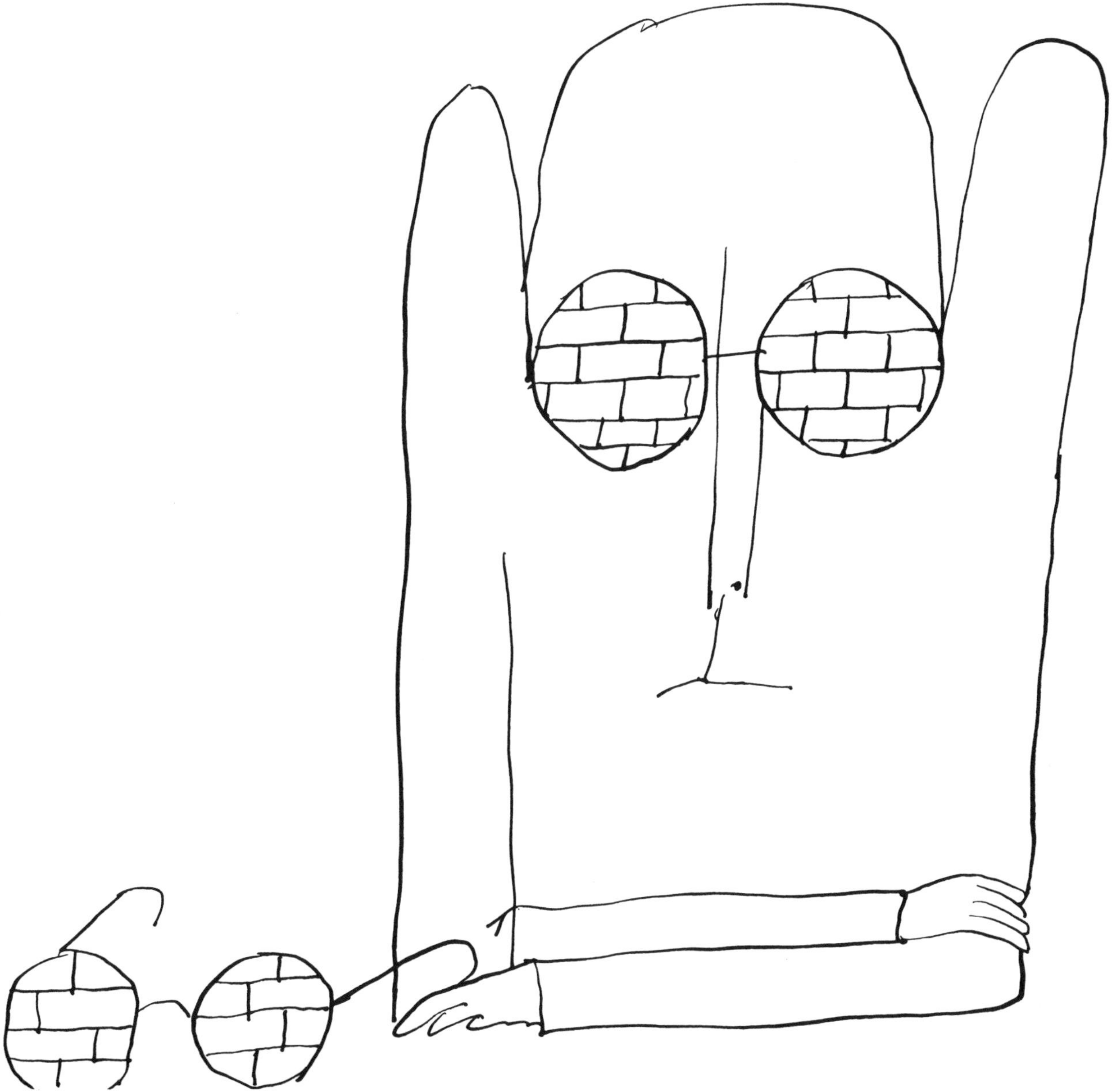

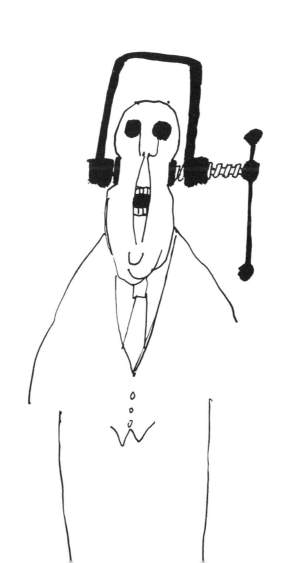

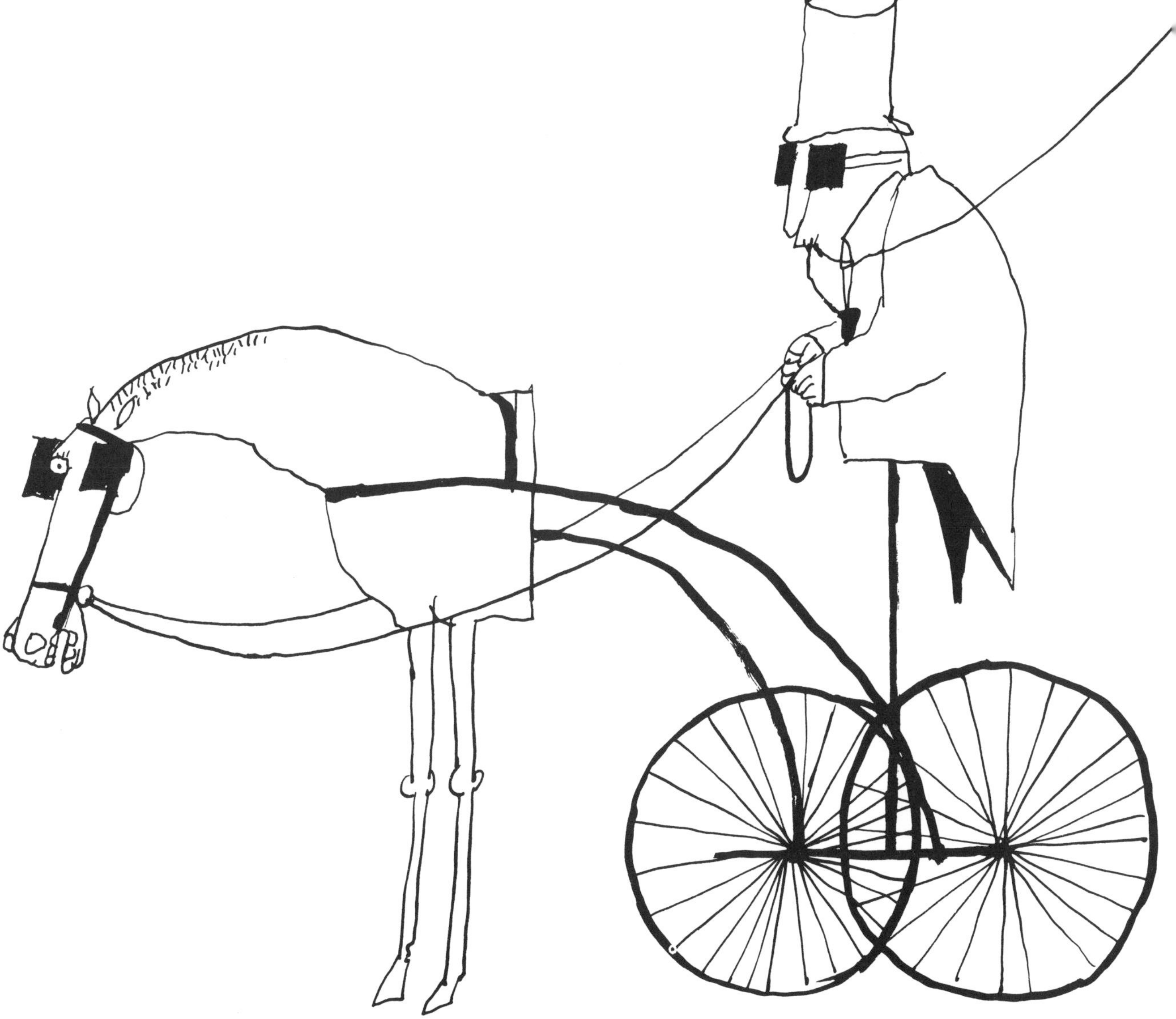

the applicant

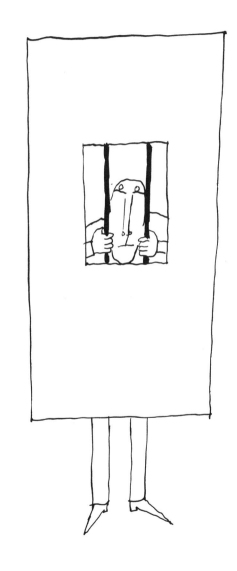

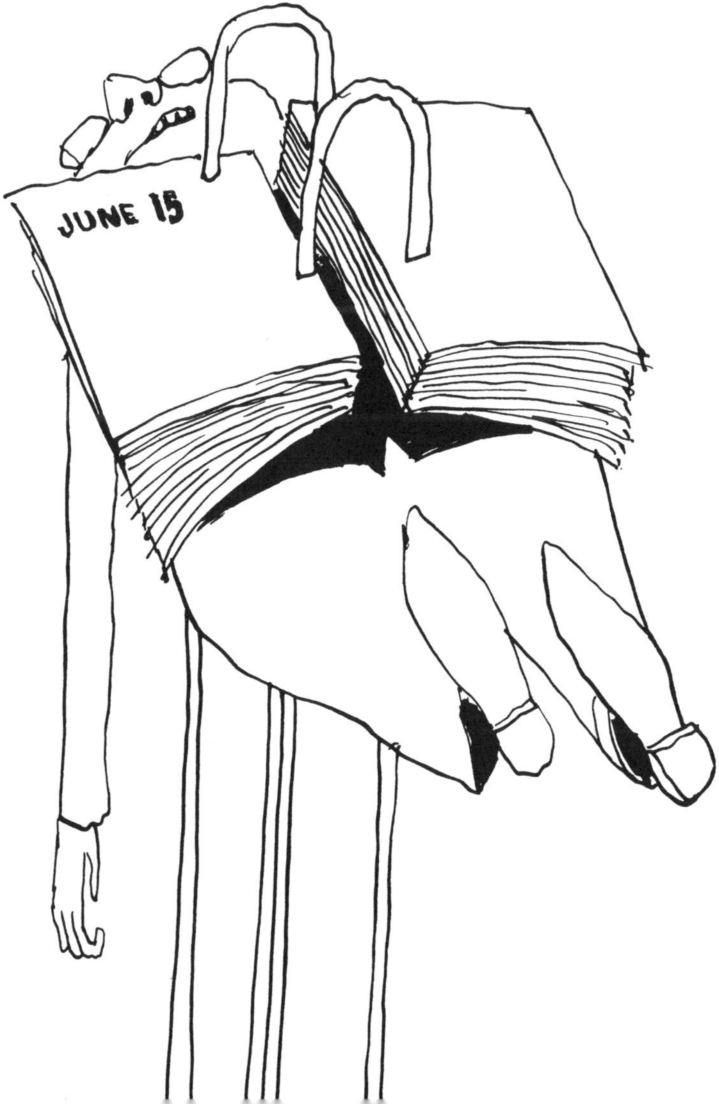
JUNE 15

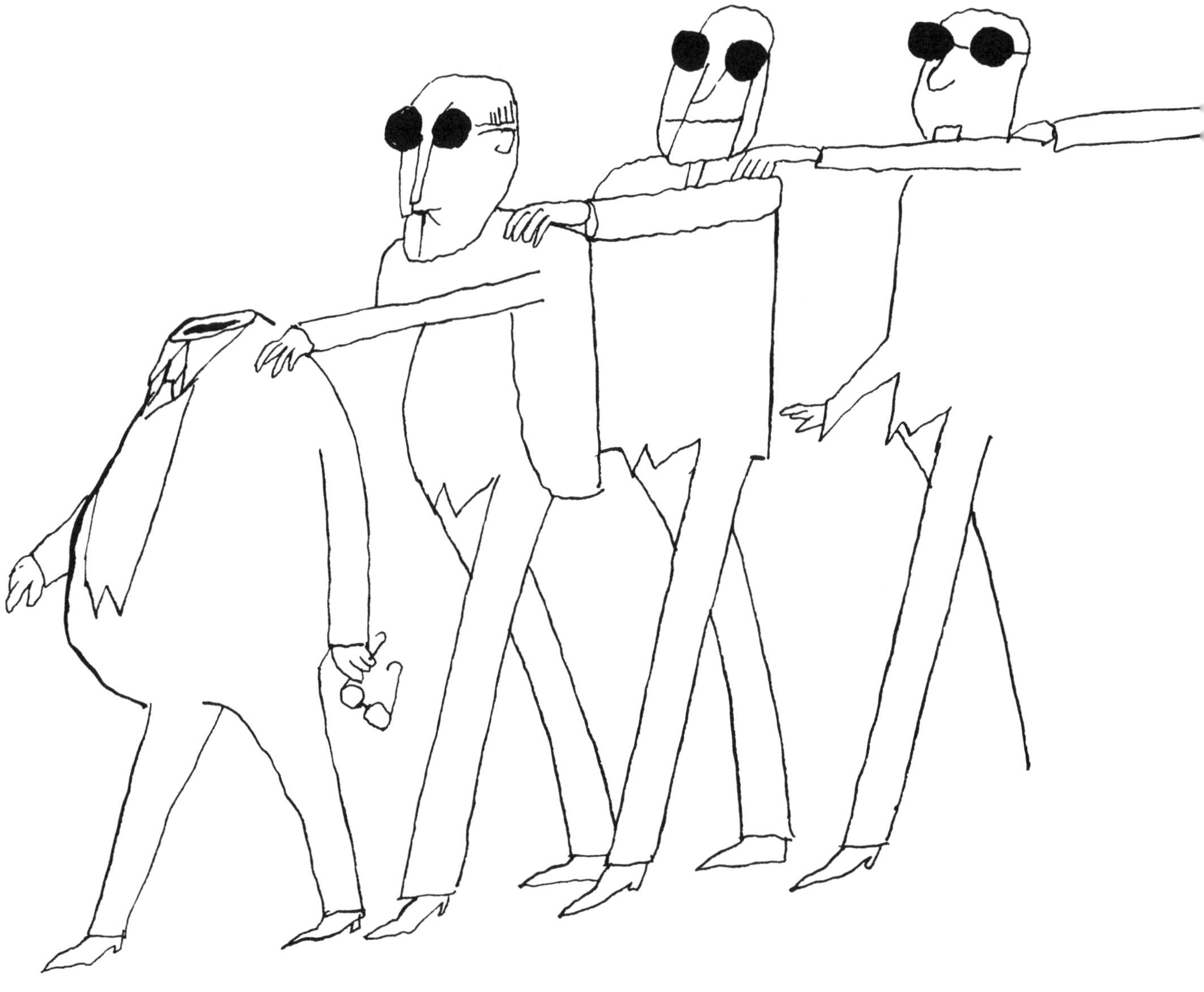

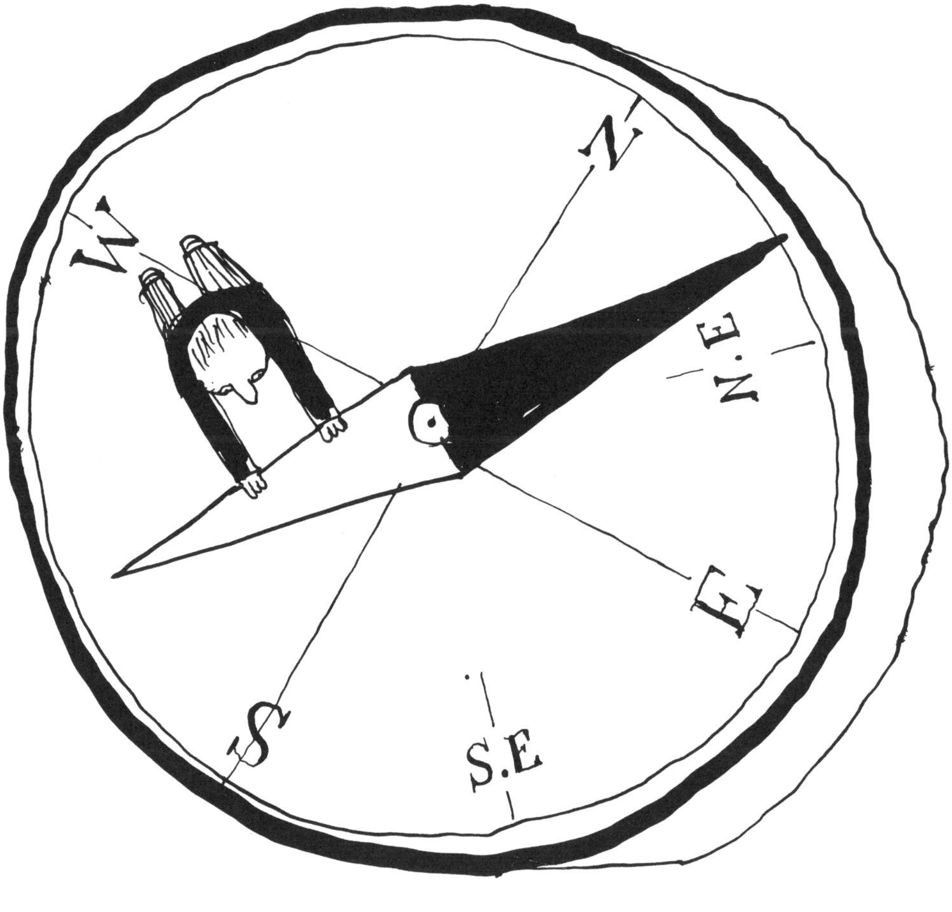
N
W
N.E
E
S
S.E

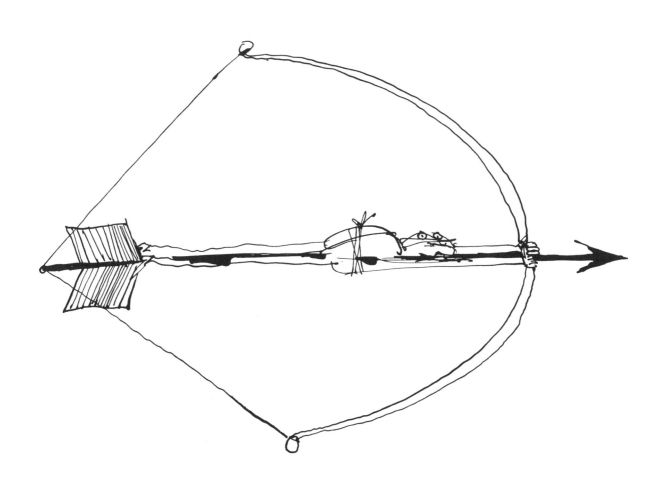

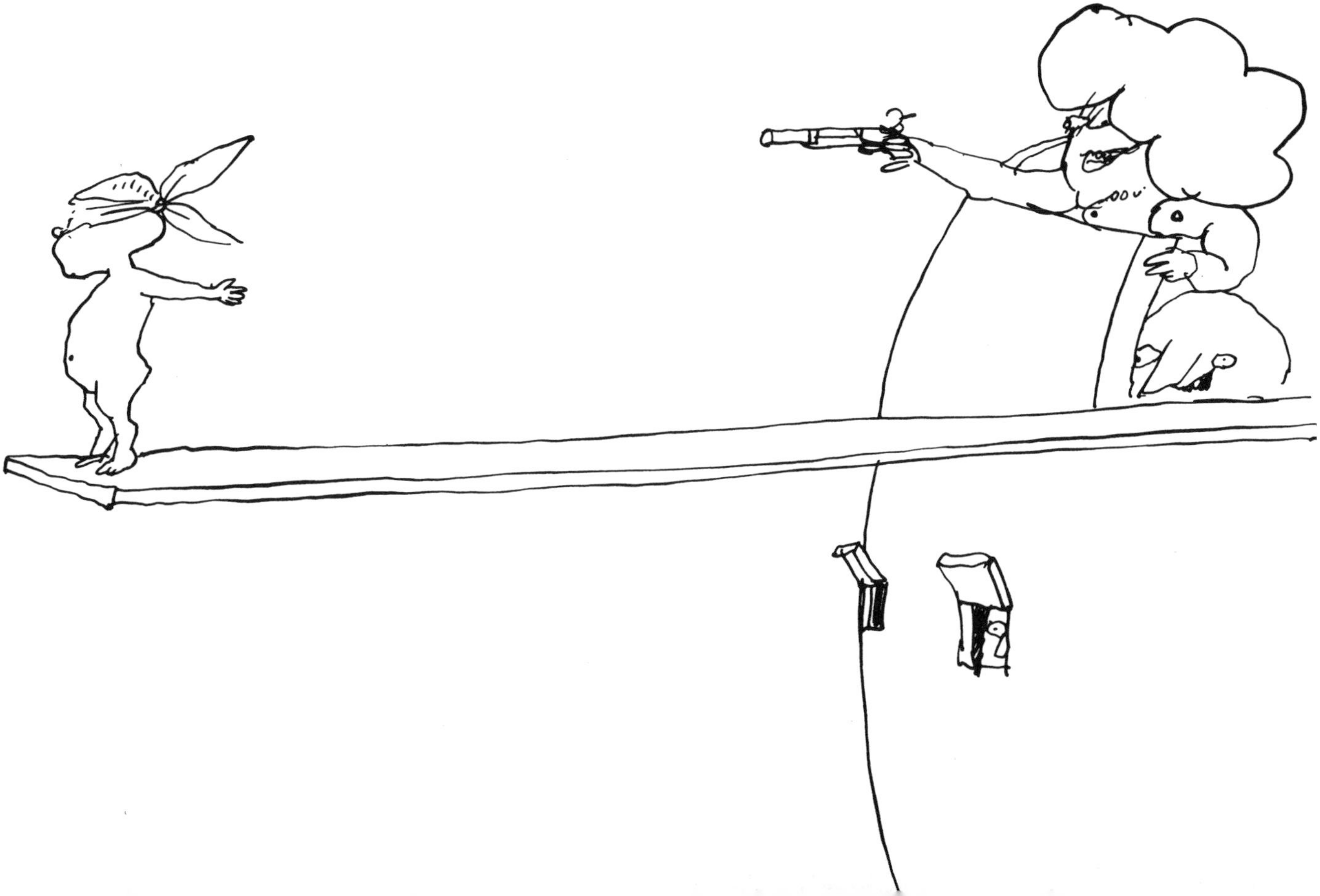

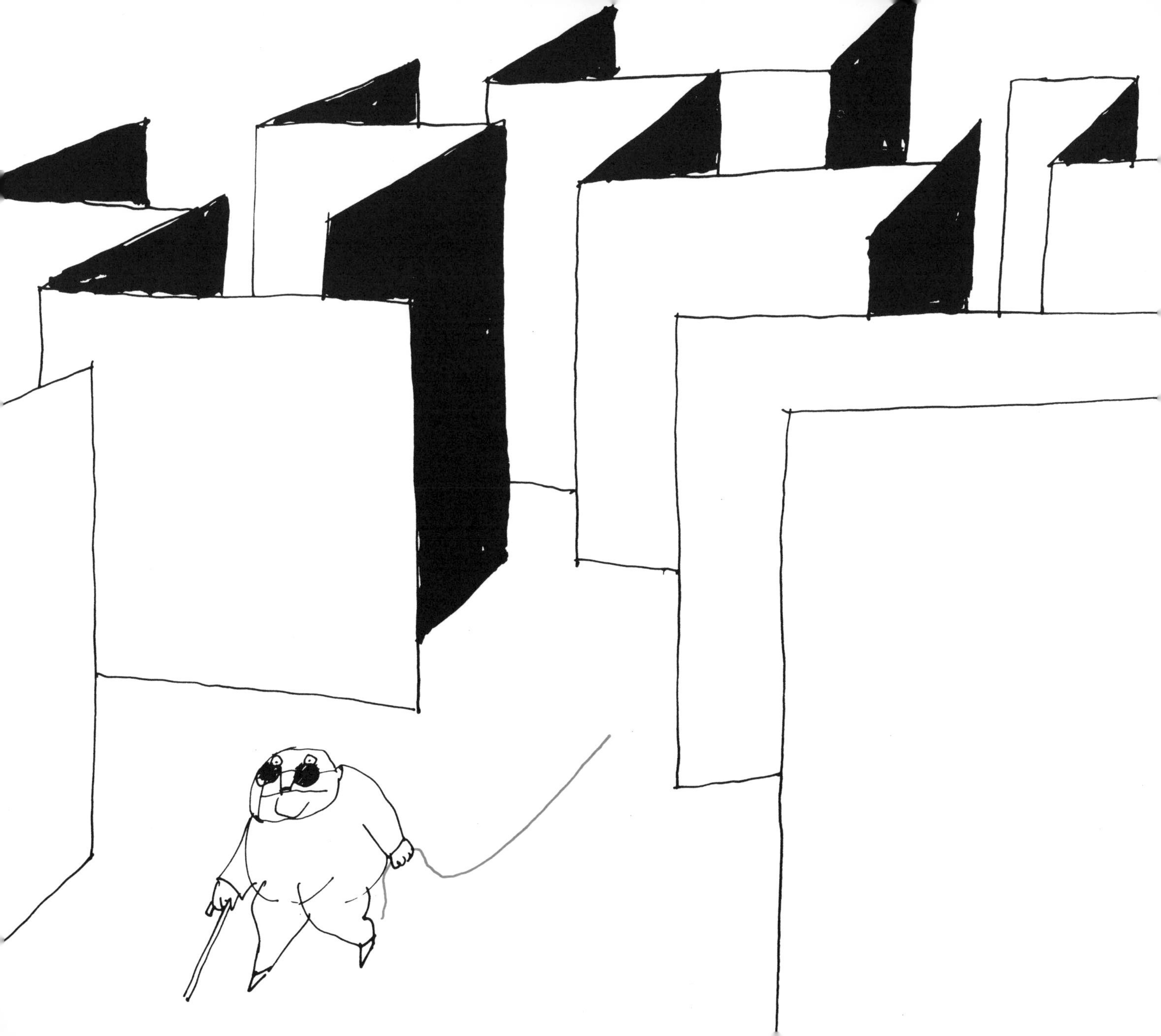

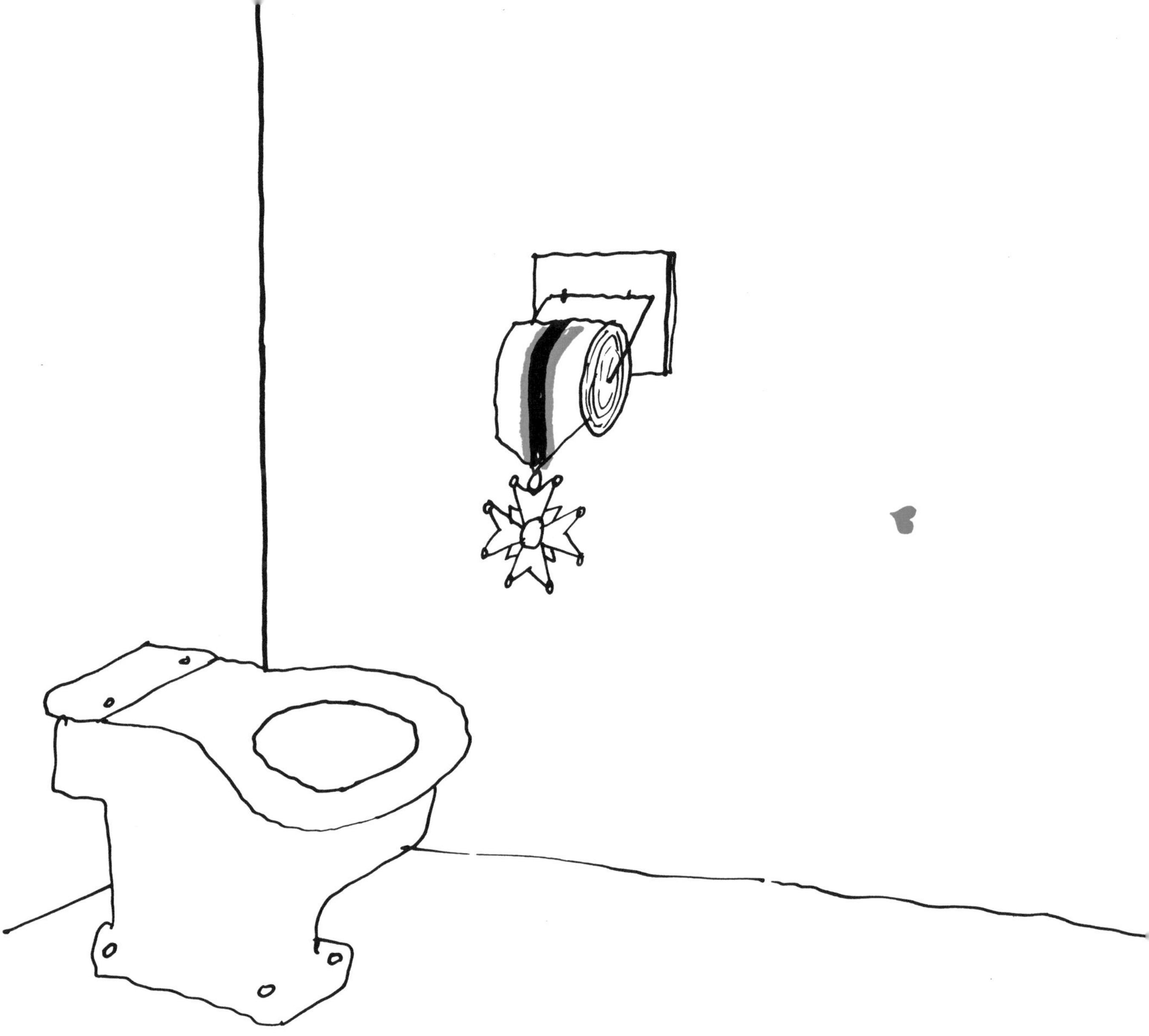

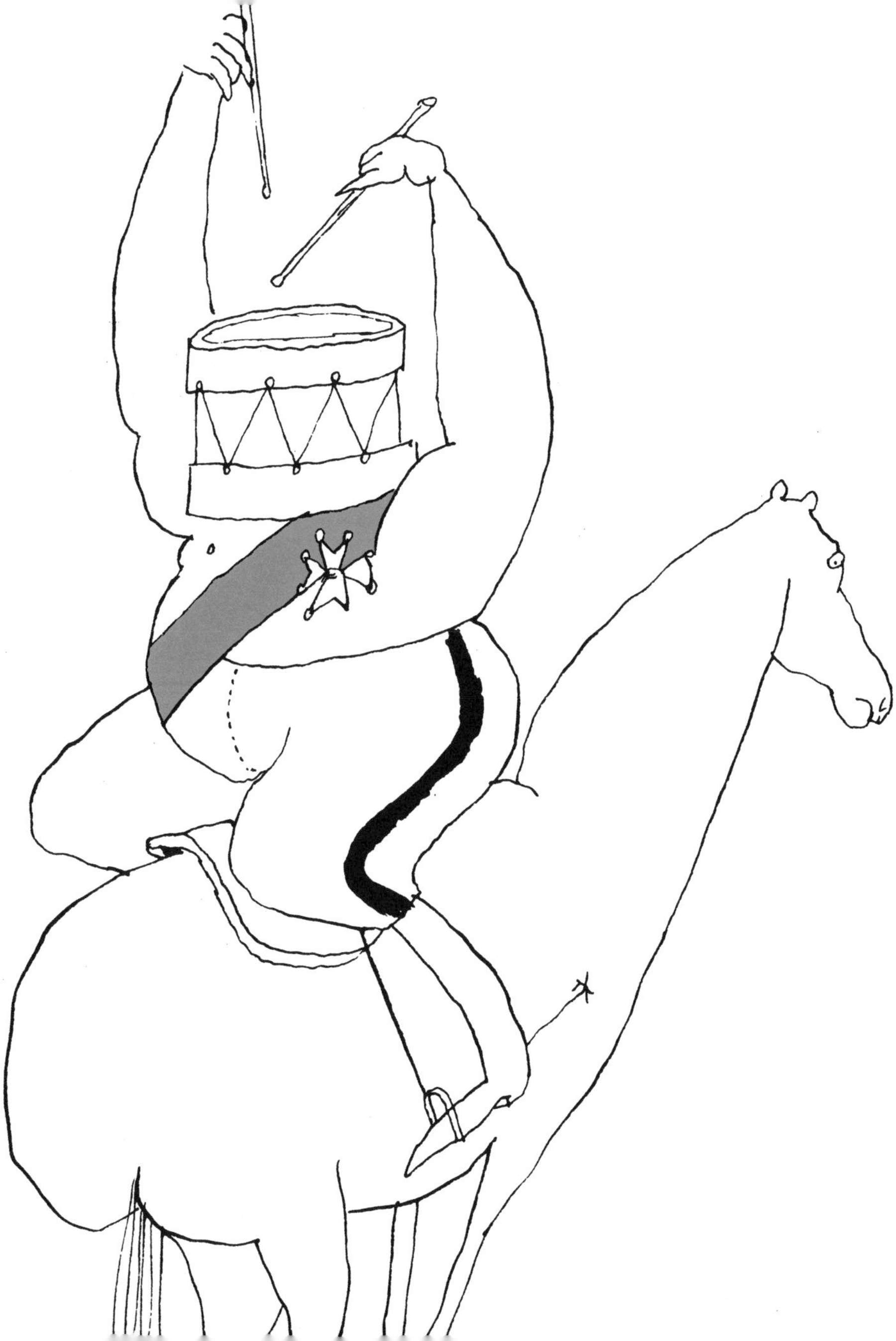

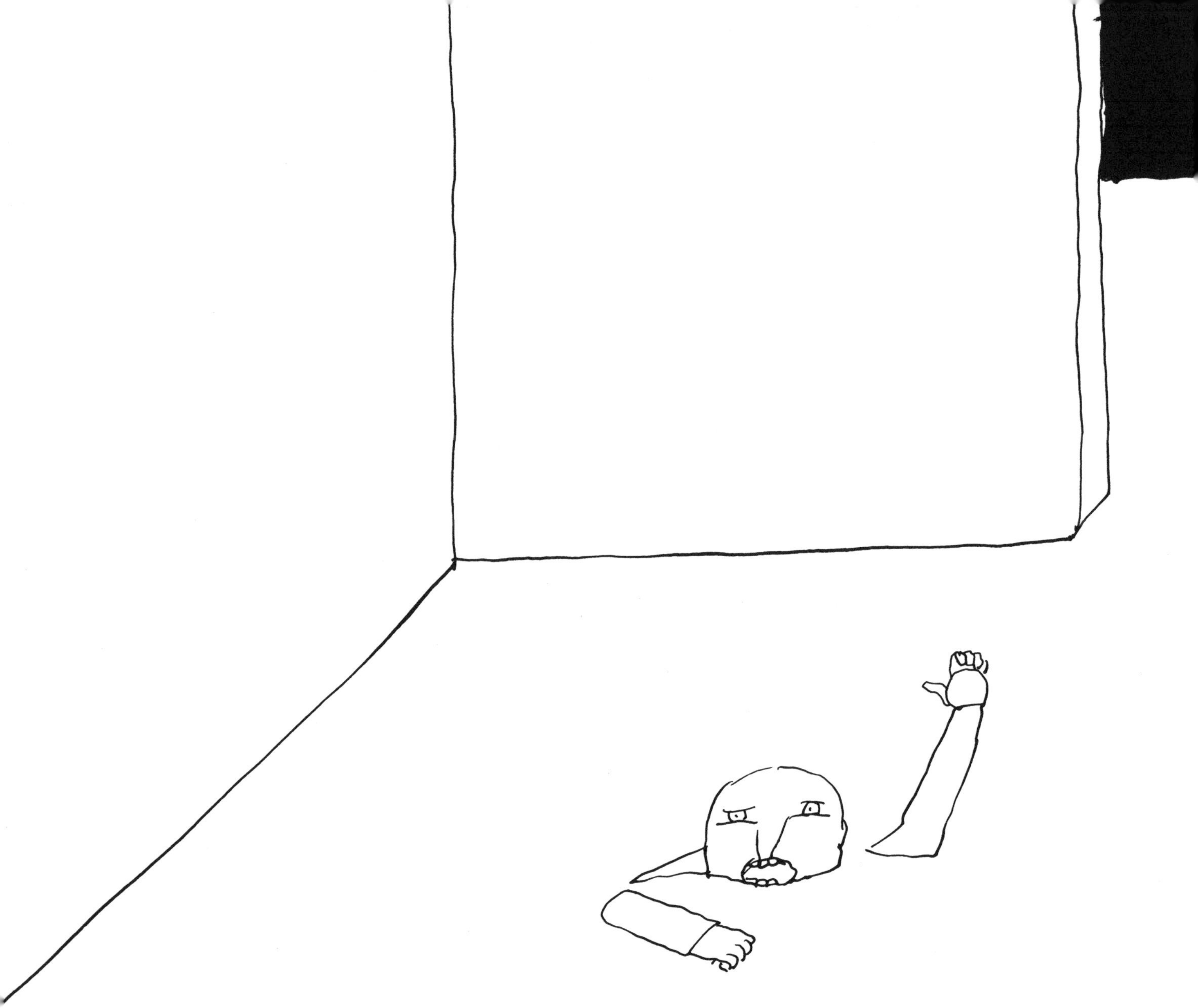

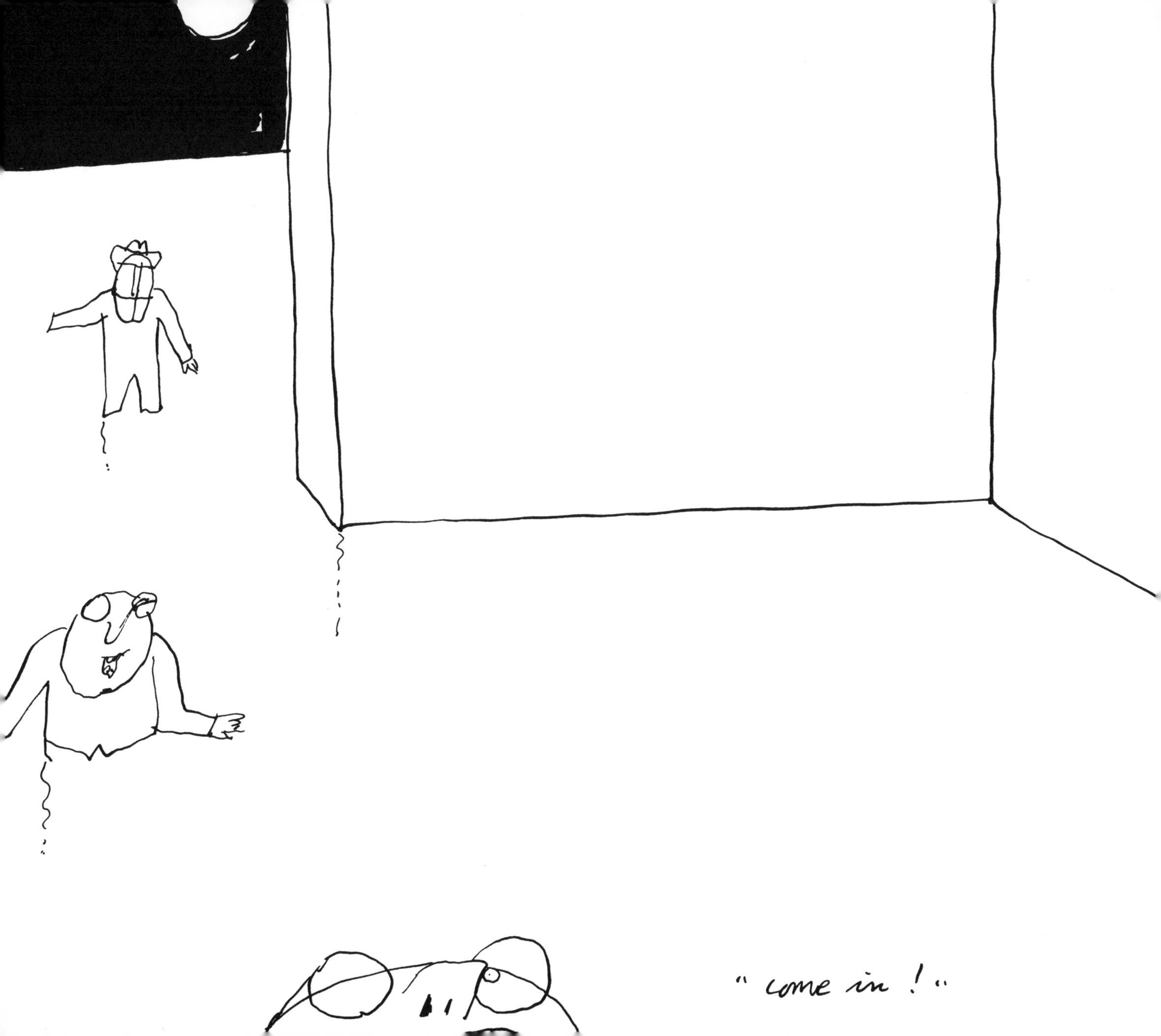
" come in ! "

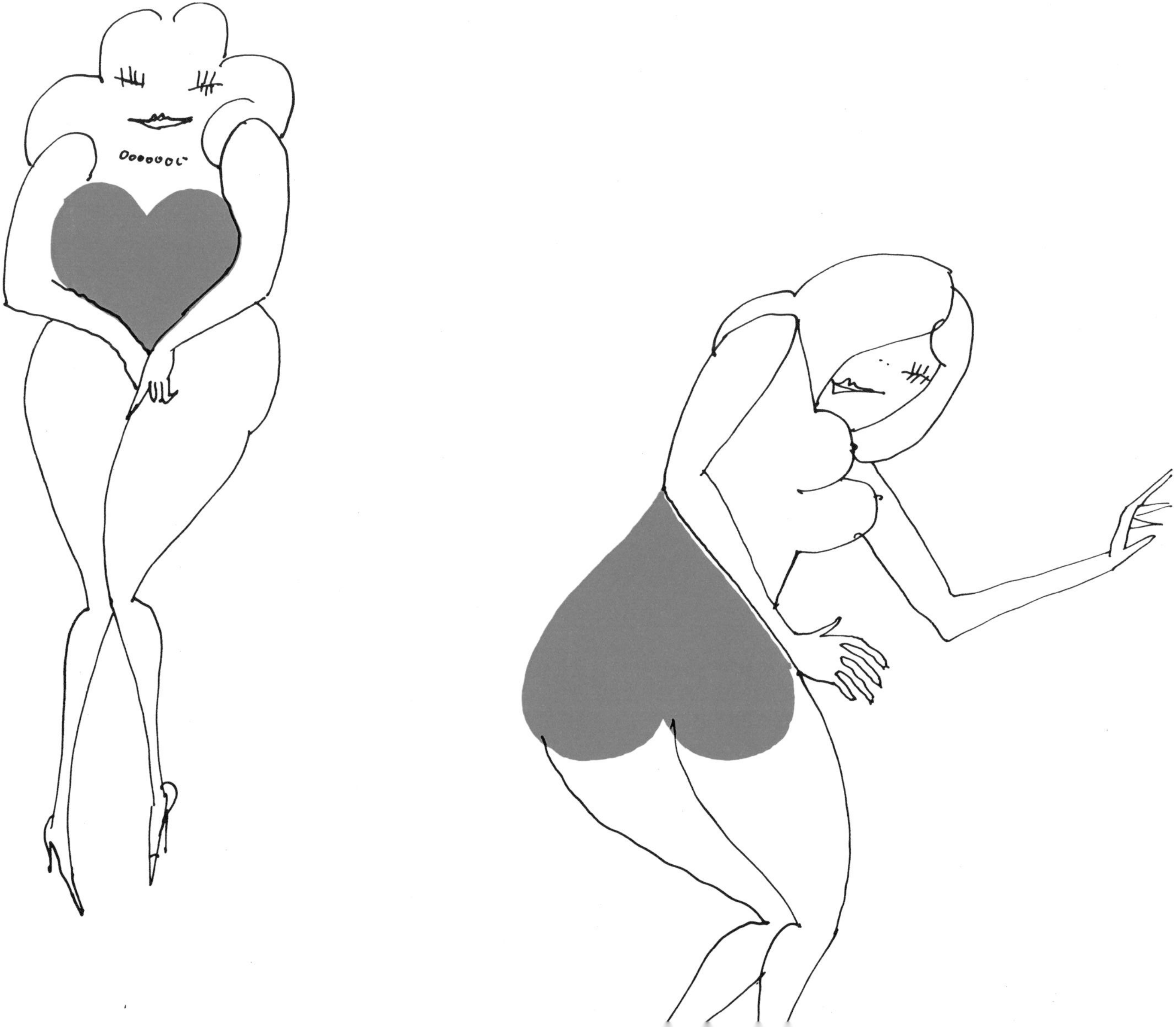

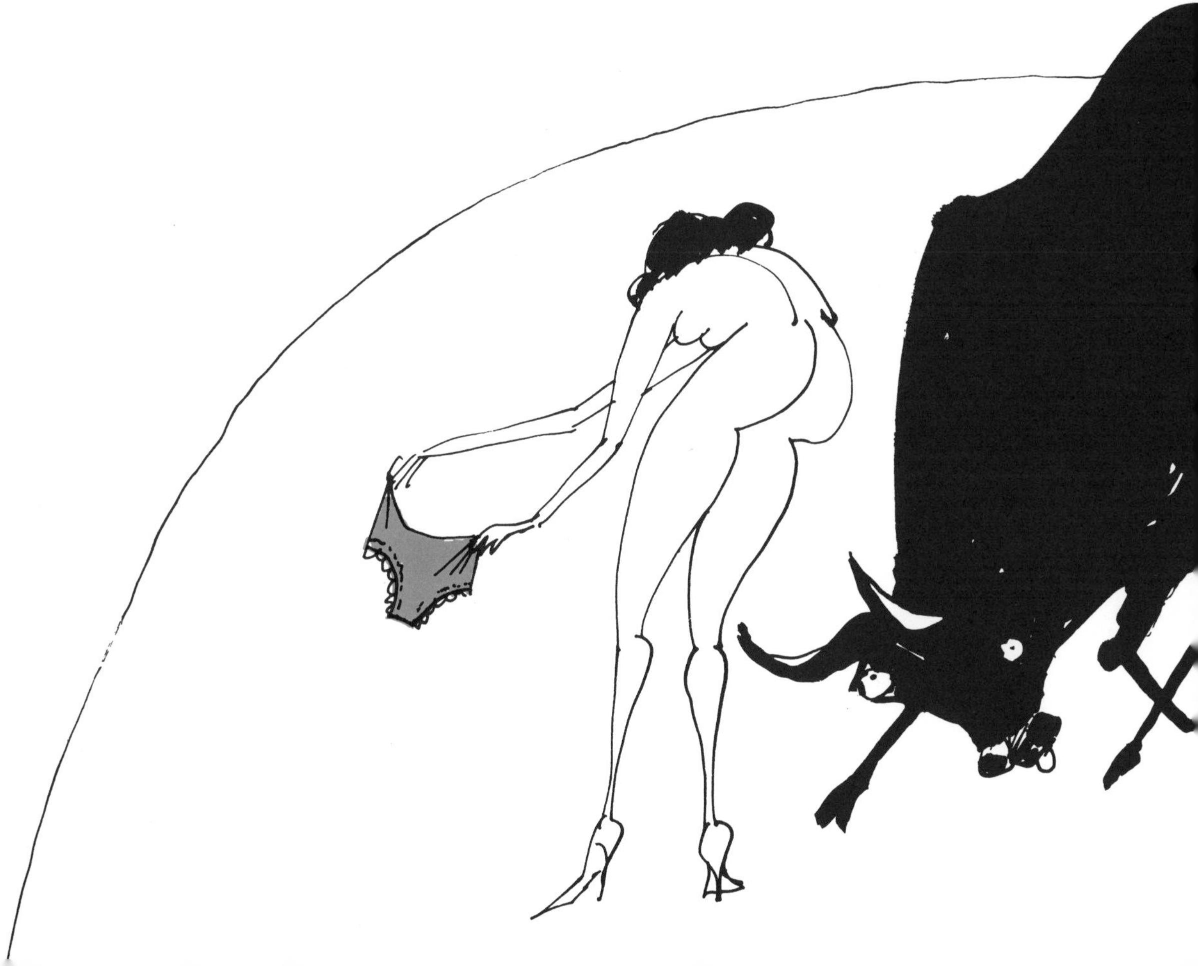

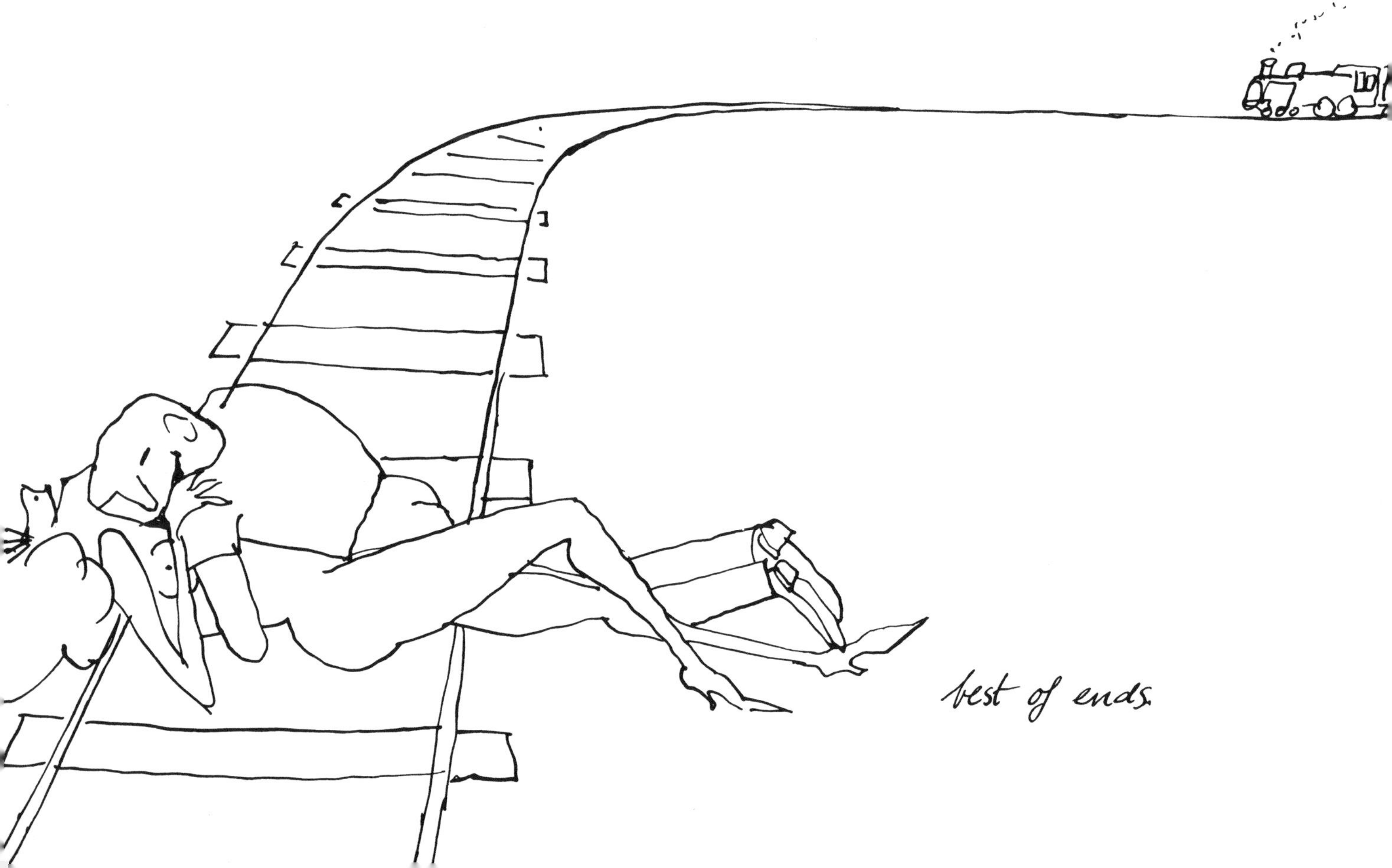

best of ends.

end

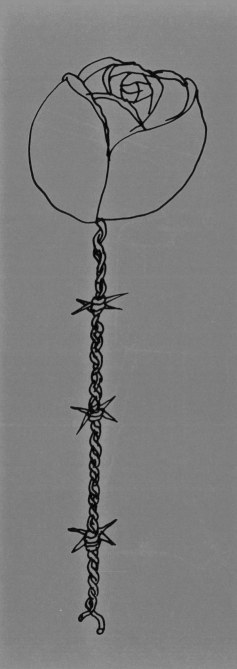

Editor: Gary Groth
Design: Ungerer and Covey
Production: Preston White
Associate Publisher: Eric Reynolds
Publisher: Gary Groth

*The Underground Sketchbook* is published by Fantagraphics Books. First published in 1964 by Viking Press, Inc., New York. Copyright © 1968 by Diogenes Verlag AG Zuruch. This edition's design is copyright © 2019 Fantagraphics Books, Inc. Introduction is copyright © 2019 Steve Brodner. All rights reserved. Permission to reproduce content must be obtained from the publisher.

Fantagraphics Books, Inc.
7563 Lake City Way NE
Seattle, WA 98115

ISBN: 978-1-68396-262-5
Library of Congress Control Number: 2019933501
First Fantagraphics Books edition: February 2020
Printed in Hong Kong